DIVAS
Unchained

DIVAS
Unchained

Women & Girls Breaking Free
from Statistics & Strongholds

Dr. Nioka Smith

J. Kenkade
PUBLISHING®

Little Rock, Arkansas

J. Kenkade Publishing
6104 Forbing Rd
Little Rock, AR 72209
www.jkenkadepublishing.com

J. Kenkade Publishing is a registered trademark.
Printed in the United States of America.
ISBN 978-1-955186-12-4

This book recounts actual events in the life of Nioka Smith according to the author's recollection and perspective. While all the stories and testimonies in this book are true, some of the names and identifying details may have been changed to respect the privacy of those involved. Any resemblance to actual persons, living or dead, or actual events is purely coincidental.

For my daughters,
Kennedi and Kadence
& the women and girls all across the world.

"Just when I had decided to become abstinent, I found out I was becoming a statistic."

—Dr. Nioka Smith, "DIVAS Unchained"

Praise for DIVAS Unchained

"Every woman and girl should read DIVAS Unchained. Your breakthrough/deliverance may very well come."
-M. Gillam

"It takes courage to write about your own struggles, but most of all, the entire world of women's struggles. Dr. Nioka continues to set standards and pave the way for others."
-N. Covington

"I have decided to re-read the book! I can't even put it down. As I read it, it's like I can actually hear the voice of the author. This book is taking an effect on me."
-A. Hicks

"It has touched a place in my heart that has never been touched. So many people will be unchained because of it."
-S. Drake

"I wish I could have read this book 10 years ago. A book all women and girls should read. Powerful and transparent. Thank you Dr. Nioka. I'm saving this book for my daughter."
-T. Moore

"This book is VERY ADDICTIVE. Once you start reading, it is hard to stop!"
-K. McAbee Cole

"This book is always on time! I feel EVERY WORD in it each time I read it. It was definitely Godly written. Even without talking to someone, Dr. Nioka, your story and hard work gives hope to others. The example you set is truly admirable. I'm glad he chose you!"
-A. Smith

Dear Diva Reader,

I have prayed for you. I have prayed for your freedom, healing, joy, fulfillment, prosperity, success, and the discovery of your purpose in life. I have prayed that every single lie of the enemy, pitfall, stronghold, and statistic that has been attached to your life be broken and shattered in the name of Jesus! I have prayed that what has once been a stumbling block to your hope and dreams will lose its grip and that its power be shifted into your hands so that you may be able to seize everything that belongs to you. I have prayed that every blindfold that has hindered you in the areas of your relationships, self-worth, growth, and success be removed in the name of Jesus. I have prayed for your strength to effectively apply all five virtues of the DIVAS Unchained principle that I share in this book, so that you will become unstoppable and walk right into the doors that God prepared for you long ago. I have prayed that you will walk unashamedly with God as the most powerful and authentic YOU that there will ever be in this world! I may not know you, but I see you as my sister and I love you just like a sister. Go forth my Diva sister...Become unchained!

In Sisterhood,
Dr. Nioka
(Nee-o-kuh)

CONTENTS

Preface

Spiritual Blindfolds

For the weapons of our warfare are not carnal, but mighty through God, to the pulling down of strongholds."
II Corinthians 10:4

ᔐ

Women and girls are under attack like never before! Satan places a plethora of strongholds in our minds so that he can keep us from the truth, keep us from success, and keep us from what God has for us. There are so many women and girls who are completely unaware that they are hostage to their situations, so they have no strategies on how to break the destructive cycles that they are in. Oftentimes, women and girls cannot even see the harmful cycles that are repeated in their lives. This is because the stronghold places a spiritual blindfold on them and manipulates the way they think and perceive things. The unemployed, unsupportive, or unfaithful men that they keep attracting; the deadbeat fathers that they keep having children by; the continuous failed relationships with men; the loss of jobs or inability to land a satisfying career; the financial dead-ends; the unreached goals; the in-and-out of depression stages; the lingering guilt and shame from a past event; the excessive "never getting ahead", one step forward and three steps back; and the constant brutal confrontations and brawls with women—all constitute destructive cycles in a person's life. These cycles are strongholds that Satan uses against you.

These cycles/strongholds are designed to destroy you and keep you bound.

Sadly, many of us as women and girls are reduced to a statistic—just another number.

The statistics in this book are alarming; however, we don't have to succumb to them. Throughout this book, you will see that I grew up in a very hostile environment, experienced hardships that nearly killed me, and was susceptible to much harm and demise. However, I chose not to be just another statistic. I chose not to be another number. You will see that you also have a choice to be unchained from your strongholds.

God is about to give you the power to break away from every statistic and stronghold that has attached itself to your life.

II Corinthians 10:4 tells us that our weapons against strongholds are not humanly; they are spiritual.

You cannot effectively combat these obstacles in your life with your own strength or humanly devices. The only way to effectively and permanently break the chains of statistics and strongholds is through the Spiritual power of God.

Believe it or not, Satan began planting several small seeds in your life during the time you were a little child.

The stuff we saw, heard, witnessed, and experienced as a little girl all contribute to the reasons we do things later on in our lives. The issue is that we don't realize that what happened twenty years ago has created chaos in our lives today.

Satan plants those seeds in our minds as a child, so that by the time we become adults, the small seeds grow into plants of defeat.

For so many of our women and girls, it's easier to believe that prosperity and success can happen for others, but almost impossible to see themselves in such a blessed place. God never designed you to settle for less. Throughout this book, God is about to shift your perception and empower you to go get your stuff! It's time to stop settling. It's time to go take everything with your name on it that Satan has stolen and hidden from you. It's time to snatch off the spiritual blindfolds!

Introduction

Your New Definition of Divas

Diva was originally defined by Merriam-Webster's dictionary as "a prima donna, a very successful and glamorous female celebrity; a queen or princess." Somewhere along the line, that definition of diva evolved into more definitions. Today, there are many different variations of the word diva.

Take note: The word Divas as discussed in this book does not apply to the above definition or any of the other variations in the world today. In a society that's forever changing; sometimes, we must redefine our own personal worlds in a way that makes it more suitable for us to thrive in. That's what I've done with the word "DIVAS". I want to challenge you to look at the word diva in a new light to help you to survive and thrive in this world. "DIVAS" is an acronym that God placed in my Spirit to stand for Dignity, Inspiration, Vision, Achievement, & Sisterhood. These are the five virtues that I will discuss in this book.

For the purposes of this book and for your new outlook on life, the new definition of DIVA(s) is
> "a well-rounded female(s) clothed with dignity, inspiration, vision, achievement, and sisterhood."

The Holy Spirit has instilled a message in me that will empower you to come out of your captivity and break free from darkness. This book will empower you to begin living a full life that God has planned for you. In my "Diva to Diva" sections, you will hear real life stories about women, teenage girls, and very personal testimonies from my own life experiences. I will provide you with life changing tools that God gave me to not only make it through tough times, but to victoriously overcome what seems impossible. More importantly, you will hear what the Lord wants to say to you about your current position in life, the new place that He wants to take you to, and how to get there. You will be inspired to evaluate your life as it is and be empowered to grow in your areas of weaknesses.

There is also a follow-along workbook that matches this book. The title is "DIVAS Unchained Interactive Workbook" and can be purchased at drniokasmith.com or jkenkadepublishing.com. It includes "Diva Challenges" filled with activities and exercises that will provide you with hands-on tools that are applicable to your personal life. Whether you read this book alone or with a group, Divas Unchained will empower you to win! Ultimately, God is the author, and I am just the messenger.

Grab a pen and highlighter. Your Father in Heaven is sovereign. He is ready to expose and tear down the strongholds in your life and elevate you to new levels. No matter what your current dilemmas tell you, you were created to win, there is more out there for you, and it's time for you to walk in the power that God has given you and excel in every area of your life! Declare aloud the following statements to yourself:

I am not just another number in the pool of statistics!
I will no longer succumb to the strongholds against my life!
I am a Diva…Unchained!

Dignity Inspiration Vision Achievement Sisterhood

Diva(s)
/de-vuh/ /de-vuhs/
noun

a well-rounded female(s) clothed with dignity, inspiration, vision, achievement, and sisterhood

Unchained
/uhn-cheynd/
Verb. Past tense.

to have broken free from the chains of statistics and strongholds against a Diva's life.

Stronghold
/strông-hōld/
Noun.

a place in your mind that is orchestrated by Satan, armed by his demons, and designed to manipulate the way you think and perceive things.

Author's Note:

I coined this new Diva(s) definition with the guidance of the Holy Spirit. It is my God-inspired belief and practice that when a woman or girl comprehensively possesses the five virtues that I've outlined in this book, she becomes a force to be reckoned with in the world. She will prosper in every area of her life because these five virtues constitute a very well-rounded woman. When possessing all five DIVA virtues, she will live a complete life of balance, fullness, fearlessness, and abundance.

VIRTUE ONE

The 'D' In DIVAS

DIGNITY

"A way of appearing that suggests seriousness and
self-control; the quality of being worthy of honor
or respect"

Key Bible Scripture

*"For God bought you with a high price.
So you must honor God with your body."
~I Corinthians 6:20 NLT*

1

Character Check

❧

I know that society has taught us not to care what others think, but what happens when what they think about us is true? Believe it or not, everybody is not jealous and everybody is not "stuck up" & "bougie". Sometimes, what they say about us is the truth whether we like what they say or not. There is a remarkable difference between being confident with who we are and being conformed to who society says we are. I hear many women and young ladies justify their behavior by saying they are just confident with who they are and won't change their ways for anybody. It is true that you should be confident, but you should not be a conformist! Women say things like:

"I'm me and I'm gonna do me regardless!"

"If you don't like what you see, then stop looking!"

"I'm just confident with who I am."

Watch out because what you think is confidence may just be conformity. Those who say they do not care about what others think often do so to justify their lack of dignified behavior. Let's take a look at the differences between confidence and conformity.

Being confident with who you are means being secure with any flaws or imperfections you may have. When others say you are too skinny or too fat, too dark or too light, confidence says you are God's craftsmanship and that you are fearfully and wonderfully made. Confidence means knowing who God says you are, believing it, and owning up to it no matter what others say or think.

On the other hand, being conformed to what the world says we are means living up to the opinions of others. It's when we allow their opinions and predictions to shape our behavior. Simply put, being conformed is when we make the general stereotype a personal reality. People normally expect women who live in underprivileged neighborhoods to reduce themselves as sex objects to men and on social networks.

They expect girls from poverty-stricken neighborhoods to have no "class", no dignity, and to refrain from furthering their education. They expect girls from single parent households to become teenage mothers and wear clothes that reveal their body parts.

Being conformed is when you adapt your thinking and behaviors to that of others with a similar background. It means meeting the standards that people say a person from your background should meet. Romans 12:2 says, "Be not conformed to this world, but be transformed by the renewing of your mind, that you may prove what is that good, and acceptable, and perfect, will of God." You see, when you do the things that women your age and race do just because they are doing them, you are conforming to the world. Moreover, I want you to understand that when you do things that statistics and stereotypes predict, you are conforming to who society says you are.

When we as women and girls yell in public, curse people out for looking at us the wrong way, drink and curse more than the average man, and wear clothes that reveal our sacred body parts; we are not being confident with who we are, we are *conforming* to what stereotypes say we are. When we wear hair rags and house shoes in public, fight other women, refuse to read anything other than social media drama, speak and write with poor grammar skills, and spend more money on our hair, nails, and purses than on our education, savings account, and personal growth, we are conforming to the world's expectations of us.

By conforming to stereotypes, we become a statistic...just another number.

When we behave in the manners discussed above, we are not walking in dignity; neither are we being confident with who we are. We are being conformed to who the world says we are. We are being exactly what they want us to be or what they expect us to be based on our financial, cultural, or social backgrounds. Let's stop affirming their expectations of us! As you read the next few pages on conforming to statistics and stereotypes, I admonish you to check your character to see if your actions are a result of confidence or conformity.

Your Reputation

If you were to ask five people to describe your character, what do you think they would say? Contrary to what many believe, we should care about what people say in relation to our reputation. Of course, if we are doing right by God and behaving in a way that His word says, then we don't have to worry about pleasing anyone but God. When we do what is pleasing to God, our reputation automatically falls in line with God's will. However, a female who always posts pictures on social networks, bending over showing her butt, probably has a reputation of one with very little dignity and one who is "easy" when it comes to guys.

There is not a day that goes by that I do not see a woman on Social Media where her profile picture is one where she is facing backwards and all you can see is her backside. It is one hundred percent obvious to everyone that her sole reason for posting a picture of her backside is to bring attention to her butt. It's her advertisement. She has placed her body on the advertisement menu.

A woman or girl who speaks more about her butt and how thick she is develops a reputation of one who reduces herself to a sex object. She may not think this is true; she may not even have multiple sex partners, but it's the reputation she has made for herself. It is the marketing message that she has established for herself.

People will expect the same thing and maybe even less from her, but never will they expect anything more of her unless she changes her character. Many times, people who condone this kind of behavior don't know any better themselves and may have a similar reputation. Other people who do know better may not say anything to the person directly, but shake their heads and think negatively of her in private.

A woman who posts more pictures on Facebook of being in the club and at parties than pictures of spending quality time with her children has developed a reputation of a bad or inattentive mother. The truth is people don't know what she does in her spare time. It could be that she is often at ball games with her son. However, we are referring to a reputation which only applies to how you are always talking and the things that you are always seen doing. What you mainly say and do is what they will believe. Additionally, it affects how they will treat you and respond to you.

Proverbs 22:1 tells us the importance of a reputation: "A good name is to be chosen rather than great riches." Therefore, if a good reputation is important to God, it should be just as important to you.

I'm not encouraging you to walk on eggshells around people. It's more about making sure your lifestyle is one with dignity and one that's pleasurable to God at all times. Even if this takes time, God will be pleased with your continual effort to work on your character.

Diva to Diva

As I walked into the courthouse one day to pay a speeding ticket, I met a lady who looked to be in her thirties. While waiting, we engaged in small talk whereby we spoke of our ticket fees and how expensive they were. She asked me my reason for paying. I told her it was due to speeding. I also explained to her that I was done with speeding because all it takes for me is one $165 fee. She replied, "Honey, I wish my ticket was only $165! Mine is $675!" I screeched, "Goodness gracious! How fast were you speeding?"

She giggled, "Honey, my ticket wasn't just for speeding. It was also because I cussed that chick out—that officer that pulled me over. I told her about herself!"

Apparently, the lady driver was speeding and happened to have one of her headlights missing. The woman argued with the police officer by saying she was "picking" on her and discriminating against her. She went on to tell the police officer that she would not have noticed her headlight was missing if she had not pulled her over without a reason. She said she questioned the officer for pulling her over and put her "in check".

In other words, she let the officer know just how wrong she was and that she was not intimidated by the female officer. The woman driver resisted cooperation with the officer and called her out of her name. This led to more citations that the officer added such as no seatbelt and something dealing with insubordination to the officer.

⁂

Respect for Authority

Now, there are several issues I'd like to point out with this scenario; however, we will only discuss a few that pertain to the driver's character. First, the driver did not give the officer any respect for her authority. No matter how wrong the police officer may have been (if she was wrong), she is still in authority. The Bible tells us to respect all authority even if they are cruel and unfair because God will reward us; especially if we suffer for His name's sake—for doing what's right (1 Peter 2:13-21 NLT). When your character is so out of line that you blatantly disrespect authority, you are destined for consequences by God and the law. The fact that the driver had to "check" the police officer shows that she has no respect for authority.

There is no employer that wants to hire someone with no respect for authority. There is no person that wants to give a positive referral for someone with no respect for authority. There is no man that wants to marry a woman with no respect for authority. Instead of putting the officer in check, she should have put her character in check.

Authority is necessary for the world to function. God knew it was important which is why it was written in the Bible. I know a lady that was fired from every job she has ever had because she hated authority. She said no one was going to tell her what to do! She said she will be unemployed for the rest of her life before someone tells her what to do and works her like a slave.

Well, that's the very reason this lady is now in her fifties, still struggling every day to make ends meet, and never able to pay her utility bills on time. Please make sure that respecting authority is somewhere in your character. Yes, authority figures are out of line all the time, but there is an appropriate way to handle it.

The Fire in Your Tongue

Next, the driver of the car didn't know how to hold her tongue. Even if the police officer was being dirty and evil, there is a time to speak and a time to be quiet—even as an adult. A woman who always says things as soon as they come to her head has little or no self-control. Self-control is one of the fruits of the spirits that the Bible requires of us (Galatians 5:22-23). I know too many women and girls who think they just *have* to say something because the other person is wrong.

They have to let it out— get something off their chest. They have to make it known that they know what the other person is doing; give them a piece of their mind!

This woman that was pulled over got herself in much more trouble just because she didn't know how to hold her tongue. People whose character is made up of little self-control never seem to care much for the consequences of their tongue. "The tongue is a small thing that makes grand speeches. But a tiny spark can set a great forest on fire. And the tongue is a flame of fire! It is a whole world of wickedness, corrupting your entire body. It can set your whole life on fire, for it is set on fire by hell itself" (James 3:5-6 NLT).

Wow, the tongue is dangerous!

This does not mean that you are to be a pushover. Not by a long shot! God doesn't encourage that either. However, you must know when it's time to stop talking. In my case, I politely informed the cop that I did not have time to slow down due to the abrupt change in the speeding limits. After I saw that the cop was not in agreement, I just apologized for speeding and stopped talking. I was in enough trouble already. Truthfully, there were other things that he could've written me up for. I'm sure he would have if I had not controlled my tongue.

Now, what is the difference between the two scenarios with the woman at the courthouse and me?

We were both speeding, but one of us received a ticket for $165 and the other for $675. The difference is self-control and respect for authority. The other woman gave the police officer reason to find more things on her and to hold her accountable for them. I was in the wrong with more than speeding just like she was.

However, I controlled my tongue so the police officer showed me favor. It's not that the officer was wrong for writing the woman up for the missing headlight. However, the officer may have shown her favor for those things if the woman had just practiced some self-control and respect for authority.

If the tables were turned and I behaved as the lady at the courthouse, I'm sure the police officer would not have pardoned me! I could have faced more than double what I was already paying.

The sad part is that this lady felt like she had won. She was giggling when she told me because she was able to curse the officer out. She put the officer in "check" and told her the reason she pulled her over was because she had nothing better to do than to harass her. In her mind, she had won because she proved that she doesn't *bow down* to anybody.

It's so silly because she did not hurt the police officer at all! She ended up hurting herself and her pockets. I'm sure she was soon behind on bills and kids ended up having to suffer financially as well. However, she was too busy within her lack of self-control and lack of respect for authority that she could not even see how she defeated herself with her own tongue! Be wise! Don't set yourself up for failure. Put your character in check and control your tongue!

Confidence or Conformity?

Can you see how the woman in the above scenario conformed to stereotypes? People expect very little dignity out of a woman who was raised with one parent in the household, a girl who has no father in her life, a woman who was the product of a teenage pregnancy, a woman from the projects, a girl from a poor family, or a woman whose parents did not graduate high school.

Even if none of these fit, then there is definitely one category that fits. That is the category of the racial stereotype which says how society expects you to behave based on your race. This does not mean that every person who believes in stereotypes is racist. It means that it's the stigma placed on your race. If you conform to these demeaning statistics, you will continue to be viewed in that particular manner. If you want to prosper more in life, adapt your character to the way you would like to be perceived.

The Ugly Truth

Is society wrong for expecting these things about us and assuming them to be true? Just because we are of a certain race, come from a particular neighborhood, or a dysfunctional family, does that mean they should predict these things about us?

They shouldn't judge a book by its cover, right? Correct. However, even when we are wrong about a book and have assumed a book to be awful based on its cover doesn't change the fact that the cover of the book was awful. The truth is that the cover of the book was unattractive and did not prove itself worthy of our attention.

The cover of the book is what gives us a glimpse of what the book may be about. As such, the way you carry yourself is the cover of your book. The way you speak, dress, and behave is what gives others a glimpse of what you are about. Likewise, sometimes the covers of our books do not do us any justice. Our covers can make us or break us in this world. However, the ugly truth is we all have stereotypes of others, regardless of our race or gender. It is up to you to make sure that the cover of your book (how you present yourself) matches who you really are or who you aspire to be.

The ugly truth is that our behavior keeps the stereotypes and statistics alive! We must get to the point to where we stop conforming to these demeaning stereotypes and take a stand.

It's time to stop blaming other races and other people for our positions in life. We must get to the point where we admit that our character can act as a barrier that stands between us and our success. When we learn better, it is up to us to do better. If we choose to ignore it, we choose to stay where we are.

Your present character is linked to your future success. How do you expect others to trust or respect a woman that doesn't even respect herself enough to dress with dignity, speak with good sense, hold her tongue, and value her reputation? I say to you my sister: if you are going to conform to the stereotypes, then be ready to suffer the consequences that come along with the stigmas. I urge you to get tired of the consequences, get fed up with your lack of progress, and put your character in check!

2

Girl Exposed

‰

Coca-Cola body. Stout Junt. Dime Piece. Apple Bottom. Thick with it. Badonkadonk. Banging Body. A whole snack. Dragging that wagon. Do any of these phrases sound familiar? These are titles that men and women use to describe a woman's body when she has a big butt, big breasts, thin waist line, or nice curves. A lot of men fantasize about this kind of woman. A lot of women and girls desire what she has. She fits the image that many of today's Rap and R&B songs sing about. In other words, she fits the stereotype of a sex tool. Many women seek these titles because it indicates that she is desired by men who will give her plenty of attention. The media trains our women and girls to believe that these titles define our worth. Women in commercials advertise items such as clothes, food, and cars while showing their half-naked bodies. All along, the actual thing being sold is her body more so than the product. We can't even ride around without seeing billboards where half naked women with big butts and boobs are posing seductively while holding a bottle of cologne. The subliminal message to women is that you will catch and keep a man with the perfume. Research shows that we are exposed to over 5,000 ads per day!

Can you say wow?!

This means that our minds are constantly taking in things we are not consciously aware of—things that persuade us to feel, act, and think certain ways. These advertisements in the media play on our emotions and minds and make us feel as sexy as the lady on the billboard when we dress as such. We can find more magazines whereby women's bodies are glorified than we can find on the accolades of women's intellect. *Unfortunately, society's definition of success is more defined by the curvature of a woman's body than the capacity of her mind.* Our women and girls have allowed many celebrities to define their sexiness. We have been pulled into society's definition of attractiveness.

The most recent trend involves wearing dresses that practically show the vagina and butt through a silhouette or see-through sheer fabric. Some dresses are being designed with large holes (or cutouts) that expose a woman's hips, butt, breasts, and panties. It is quickly becoming the new norm for women to wear lingerie-looking clothes in public that expose the entire breasts and vividly showcase the woman's thong. Celebrities all over started wearing this new trend to events and immediately, women and girls around the world began searching for and wearing the very same types of dresses and clothes that expose and advertise their hips, thongs, breasts, and bare butts.

Here's the thing that women don't see: Celebrities are held to an entirely different *social* standard (but, same Godly standard) than you and me. The way our society is set up, a non-famous woman and a female celebrity can wear the same types of revealing clothes. The celebrity receives praises while the non-famous woman is seen as an attention seeker and a potential booty-call with no class or dignity. Although there are several exceptions, a lot of celebrities are not positive role models.

Yet, we make them our role models by aspiring after someone who doesn't even live by the same set of social standards that we live by.

As far as relationships with men go, let's really put it into perspective: within the millions of men that desire these famous women, there are more celebrity divorces and single celebrity women than one would imagine. Women and girls fail to see this. And women follow those celebrities right into a divorce; right into a relationship with the wrong man; and right into a spiral of drama and malicious rumors about their lives.

Expose means to be open to view; something that's *not protected or shielded.* The following pages will explain how a woman is no longer protected when she exposes her body to the world.

One of the biggest strongholds Satan uses against women and girls is the deception that dressing provocatively does not harm anyone. Satan is a liar and his goal is to kill, steal, and destroy your destiny, peace, and ultimately; your soul. The belief that the size of your butt is worth more than the depth of your inner beauty is one of Satan's traps. He spins women and girls into his web of deceit so that defeat looks like success and bondage looks like freedom.

What else is there for a woman to believe? After all, women exposure is all around us—when we turn on the television, when we listen to the radio, when we drive down the road, or when we go to work or school in the mornings. When we watch those music videos where the rich, money-making celebrities are half naked, our inner psyches are persuaded that a "banging" body is associated with success and money.

Subconciously, we think, "Hey, body exposure sells."

Whether it's to get money, snatch up a man, rack up a thousand likes on social media, or a hundred compliments on her body, it gives the impression that she is winning.

Quite the opposite. Exposing your body comes with costs.

The soul becomes vulnerable for attack because you're not shielding your body physically or spiritually. Return to the previous page and re-read the definition of *expose.*

Women think, "If I have a banging body, I must showcase it for the world to see. A sexy body is what all the hype is about!"

Many women desire the titles of *Dime piece, Thick, & Stout junt* to validate their worth; however, using their bodies to gain attention from others only earns them the title of the sex object stereotype. Women who expose their bodies get temporary gains but suffer long term consequences at the expense of their souls. They lose dignity, become an object, and a statistic all so that they can achieve something that's so fickle. They typically end up with a man that mistreats them, abuses them, misuses them, or sleeps around with other women—content with being "the other woman", being number one out of two, or being one of several women.

Let's put this into perspective: In order to gain a man's attention, the woman or girl has lowered her standards, used her body as a sex object, and sacrificed her self-worth; yet, she's still not the only one.

She ends up going through the same drama repeatedly with every man she dates. She constantly wonders why men won't respect her. She has written all men off as being "no good". She continues to attract and accept the same type of men who never respect her because she feels she has no other choice. She spends several years wondering why men won't respect her without realizing that she disrespected herself *first* by exposing her body and advertising herself as a sex tool to the men.

Clothes represent one of our many advertisements. The truth

is that men treated her the way she marketed herself—not as a queen, but as a tool to use when needed only to throw back in the toolbox when finished—at least until she's needed for his use again. Women and girls often tell me that they want their future husband to treat them like my husband treats me. They see the way he wines and dines me, brags and shows the world how blessed he is to have me, is committed to me, encourages and supports me within all my endeavors, comforts me, protects me, gives me his quality time, financially provides for me, and so much more.

I tell them a woman or girl should always talk like she values her character, dress like she values her body, and walk like she values her destiny. My above quote has been said in many different ways; yet, women and girls still settle to dress in ways with the sole intention of gaining the attention of men which garners absolutely no commitment or validation of their value as a woman.

Attraction does not equal commitment; neither does it mean a man thinks you are valuable to him.

If you want a man to treat you like a queen, don't carry yourself like a sex tool; carry yourself like a queen that deserves respect and cherishment. Noteworthy men cherish and honor queens, not tools. He has no obligation to the tools; they are for his use only. But when you carry yourself as a queen, that decent man will have a desire to treat you as such. Contrary to what comes out of the mouths of women, queens do not expose their bodies! God says you are royalty (1 Peter 2:9). *Find your tiara, put it on, and then carry yourself as such.*

When you expose yourself, you oftentimes hold back your blessings because God retains many blessings until we become obedient to His word (Psalm 66:18). Another way self-exposure defeats a woman is through her children, nieces, or other family members that look up to her. Generational curses are real! Therefore, when you expose yourself, your daughter may adopt your behavior and the cycle may continue for generations. This includes the kind of men she will attract and accept. God said that He has given you a choice between life and death and blessings and curses. However, it is up to *you* to choose life so that you and your children may live life to the fullest (see Deuteronomy 30:19). The way that you carry yourself affects your children as well as your grandchildren. Just as you deserve better from a man and more blessings out of life, so do your children! I could write another book about how exposing your body causes more defeat than success. The essence of it is this: The trick of Satan is to make you believe that your entire worth is within your body parts in order to keep you blinded from all the potential that God has stored within you. I promise you were born with so much purpose within you! If Satan can keep you focused on exposing your body, you will never realize how you've become just another statistic; another number in society with no name or value.

Noteworthy men cherish and honor queens, not tools. He has no obligation to the tools; they are for his use only.

Don't get me wrong; there is nothing wrong with having a beautiful body. The problem is when women advertise their bodies as their sole source of self-worth. Our bodies are amazingly beautiful with a gorgeous design that only God could create. Although God designed us with beautiful bodies, He never intended for us to showcase our bodies as if it is the only prize we have to offer. He designed your naked body parts for your future or current husband—and him only.

A *decent* and *praiseworthy* man wants a woman who doesn't show her body parts to the world. My husband *loves* that my body is marketed for him and him only. When you showcase your body for your husband's eyes only, its only one of the few things that makes a man proud and makes him *want* to cherish you. Trust me on this. To expose our beautiful bodies is to sacrifice self-worth and to distort our focus for our life's purpose. The types of clothes you wear determine the types of guys that approach you.

Why do Guys do it?

A guy usually degrades and disrespects women who expose themselves. The truth is that guys don't respect girls who don't respect themselves. Now, here's a secret: The guy that wants a girl will never tell her that he thinks she's dumb or worthless because his main agenda is to get the girl in bed. However, he doesn't respect a lady that allows him to be with other females. He doesn't value a woman or girl that dresses slutty. Yes, he likes to look at a girl that shows her body parts. Of course, he does; it's in his nature! He's a man!

Don't mistake a man's desire for you as respect for you. Just because he desires you does not mean he respects you! Another sad truth is that half of the time, women don't even know guys are disrespecting them because they don't realize that they disrespect themselves! It is not respect when a guy whistles to you:

"Yo, lil' mama!"

"Aye Shawty. What's yo name?"

"Ooh, baby, you are thick with it!

"Can I be in between those sheets with you?"

"Dang! Look at that ass!"

"Aye baby, what's your number? You're looking sexy in those jeans!"

That is no way for a man to approach you! He is letting you know up front that he's all about the sex and that you are only a sex tool to him. So why is it that women get into a relationship with this type of guy and end up being so upset at him when he begins to curse her out, cheat on her, or refuse to help pay bills? She exposed herself as a sex object and he did not lie to her about who he was. In fact, all the red flags were there. Here's another tip: If he only talks about your body, he doesn't respect you; neither will he treat you with respect. He talks only about your body because that's how you appear to him. You glorify and over worship your body when you expose your body. It's like holding a big flashing sign up with arrows that screams, "Place all your attention here because all my value is within these areas of my body."

> ❧
> *If Satan can keep you focused on exposing your body, you will never realize how you've become just another statistic; another number in society with no name or value.*

If you are dressed in anything that reveals a lot of your body, he feels like that's what you are showcasing to him. He feels you are the type of woman that has no values or respect for herself or who has little self-worth and will accept anything. Even if he is a decent guy, he won't waste his respectful, time-consuming, husband material skills on you. You can tell if he will respect you or not by what he mainly speaks of. If he constantly speaks about your butt, vagina, thighs, or breasts, those are the things you are exposing to him. If he speaks of everything that you can offer him instead of what he can offer you, chances are he only desires you, but won't respect you.

When you dress a certain way just to get a guy's attention,

those are the kind of guys that you are going to get—either the ones who only want good sex with you and no relationship or the ones who will stay in a relationship with you, but don't know how to treat a woman right and can't catch a woman with dignity to save his life. Remember, when you dress this way, you are exposing yourself as a sex object. The definition tells us anything or anyone that is exposed is no longer protected. Therefore, your dignity and success are in jeopardy as well as your respect from other people.

About 58% of men said they become sexually aroused when women wear revealing clothes and that they believe that the woman wears the clothes to intentionally arouse them. [2]

Note: That's about 6 out of the 10 men that you walk past every day who become sexually aroused by your revealing clothing.

A *Diva* (according to the new definition of *Diva* I have given you) has dignity and doesn't diminish her standards in any way. Just because something is a trend doesn't mean you jump on the bandwagon. Come on. Let's dare to be classy Ms. Diva!

Let's stop being a stereotype and statistic. We're better than this! You don't need to expose your bodies to affirm your worth or importance. You are worthy because God says you are!

Don't claim titles to things that describe you as an object (such as a brick), an animal (such as a chick), a coin (such as a dime), a piece of fruit, or a drink. **Understand that the value you carry is too vital to be attached to such lowly things!**

You're important because you are here and have purpose brewing in you that you aren't even aware of yet.

You must learn your worth and leave some part of you up for curiosity. Allow the man to desire your mind first instead of your body parts. Allow him to be intrigued with your character and qualities first.

What sets *you* apart from all the other pretty faced, curvaceous bodied women and girls? "Charm is deceptive, and beauty does not last; but a woman who fears the Lord will be greatly praised" (Proverbs 31:30). What is your substance? You have something to offer that's beyond the tangible body and the *fading* beauty. Find out what it is! Because *that* is what the man will hold on to when all is said and done. This is what makes him desire more than your body.

A woman or girl with value, substance, and dignity makes a man desire more than her body—it makes him desire her heart and soul! Make him wonder. Advertise your substance instead of your body. Make him wait on your goods until he has earned it, until God has told you he is the one, and until marriage.

How to Carry Yourself

Don't think I'm old. I'm still young and still think that looking amazing and being fashionable is very necessary! I also know that dressing in an exposing or revealing way will prevent a young lady from ever attracting a man that would respect her. It is a definite way to attract a man that has absolutely no intentions on treating her like a queen or has no knowledge on how to treat her like a queen. Then, a woman or girl ends up wondering why she can never find a man that treats her the *right* way. It's because she continues to showcase her body as the only thing that she is worth. You cannot expect a man to treat you like a queen when you carry yourself like a sex slave.

The bible says, "I want the women to dress modestly, with decency and propriety, adorning themselves, not with elaborate hairstyles or gold or pearls or expensive clothes" (1 Timothy 2:9 NIV). What does this mean? Does this mean that God wants you to dress like a nun? No. Does God want you to refrain from wearing nice clothes? That's definitely *not* God's desire. In fact, the scripture says that you should "adorn" yourself which means to beautify and add ornaments of beauty such as jewelry. God is saying He wants you to show your beauty through dressing in appropriate clothes that are modest. Modest simply means dressing respectably and with the right amount of skin showing. If you bend over, others should not be able to see your panties or butt.

Whenever you buy clothes, you should always perform "The Modesty Test". Take time to see how you will appear to others when you actually wear the clothes. When it's a skirt or dress, try sitting down in a chair comfortably to test the modesty of it. Whatever you buy, truly think of what you will be advertising yourself as.

And by all means, save the see-through, lingerie-looking clothes for home and your husband. Keep it classy, but covered!

The Reasons Behind it All

There are reasons God wants you to dress modestly. One reason is to help you reach your destiny which was discussed earlier. In addition to protecting you and your children, God wants you to dress modestly to protect other Christians. The Bible says when you wear things that reveal your sexual body parts, you cause other men of God to stumble in their Christianity. When guys see your sexual body parts, they begin to get images in their head and wonder what else is under that garment. Make sure that whatever you do does not hinder a person's walk with God (Romans 14:21). You don't want to ever be a stumbling block for others. Your clothing could be attracting a guy that's trying to live right by God. *Newsflash: It's not just guys in your age range that you attract.* You also attract the old men, ex-convicts, and the psychotic men. So, now you have these men dreaming of you and fantasizing different thoughts about you. Even scarier, you cause the rapists and molesters to fantasize about you.

⌒

About 1 in 7 girls will be sexually abused before they turn 18. [3]

Diva to Diva

℘

Many years ago, a girl was walking home one evening in the broad daylight minding her own business. She was about sixteen years old and was not sexually active. She was wearing what we used to call "Daisy Dukes" which were very small blue jean shorts (booty shorts) that revealed a lot of skin. Although she had no intention on attracting any guys' attention, this man in his late fifties called for her to come to him. She began to walk fast and as he started following her, she walked faster and faster. Suddenly, the man caught up with her, grabbed her, pulled her into an abandoned building and raped her. He physically beat her and forced her to perform oral sex on him as well as have vaginal intercourse with her. He had taken her virginity and she didn't even have sex on her mind.

$$\wp\partial$$

Could it have happened to anybody? Yes. Was it her fault? No. Did she increase the likelihood of it happening to her? Sadly, the answer is yes. She did. She exposed herself as a girl who was sexually active by wearing "booty shorts". Even though she was not sexually active, the man surely thought she was. She had turned on his sexual radar by what she was wearing. She exposed herself; which means *not shielded or protected*. Once you turn on those signals in a guy, it's not as easy for some of them to turn it off. Sexual addictions are just as potent as drug addictions. God wants to protect you from these types of incidents. Be cute. Be fashionable. *But dress appealing without being too revealing!*

You teach a lot of people how to approach you and treat you based on what you value most. You mean more than material items. You are more than just your legs, hips, butt, breasts, and clothing. You are beautiful. You are a girl or woman of worth.

Have you ever seen the type woman or girl that has to always explain herself to others because what others think of her is totally different from who she says she really is? She's always posting pictures on Social Media where she's half-naked, turned around, or bending over to show her butt, but she constantly has to explain to people that's just the way she takes pictures; but says she's not really like that in person.

Don't be the woman/girl who constantly has to explain herself to others. What you wear is your advertisement. It is what you showcase to others as your personality and character. If you dress like a female that is "easy" and trashy, then that's who you are exposing yourself to be.

I'll tell you this truth: Guys are going to believe more of what you advertise than what you verbalize. What you expose is what they believe.

God is a jealous God (Deuteronomy 6:15), so try taking some of the energy you put into getting the attention of guys and spend it on God. Are you looking for relationship security? Jesus is a keeper! Start there. Let God guide you. The bible says, "The Holy Spirit will guide you into all truth" (John 16:13). If you truly seek God about a guy, His Holy Spirit will let you know when the right guy comes along.

He is out there! Tell God who you are interested in dating. God loves to hear when we talk to him about our desires and when we tell him what makes us smile. Does He already know? Yes! However, what He seeks is a relationship with you. That's what makes Him happy. That's what prompts Him to move on your behalf.

Women and girls focus too much on relationships with guys and forget all about God knocking on their door desiring a relationship as well. Psalms 37:4 tells us to delight ourselves in God, and He will give us the desires of our hearts. When you gain a relationship with God by praying daily and reading your bible, He will give you what you desire if it's in His will. God won't fail! He can't! Stop exposing your body. Set boundaries for yourself. Don't be so easily available. You are worth more! You are a Diva with dignity!

3

Closed Legs Don't Get Fed

Part I: Sex Disclaimer

❧

It's about to get *real*! Let's talk about sex. Whether you are an adult or a teenager, I'm sure you probably can't go anywhere without hearing something about sex. We learned in the previous chapter how the bodies of women are exposed everywhere we turn. Therefore, we know that sex talk is everywhere! You turn on the television and you hear talk about sex on almost every other channel. You turn on the radio and hear rapping and singing about sex. You go to work and there is sex talk in the break room. You go into the cafeteria at school and your peers are talking about sex. You go to a party or other social event and almost every conversation is pertaining to sex. You open a magazine and some celebrity is in there speaking about her sex life. Your Facebook timeline is filled with videos and memes about sex. You drive or ride along in a car and see a billboard that has a picture relating to sex. Sex. Sex. Sex. Women and girls hear it and see it so much that it becomes the forefront of their lives. Pre-marital sex today is just as normal as trying on clothes. Some people today are so liberated about their sex life that it is no longer a private, personal matter behind closed doors. For many women and girls, premarital sex is just a trend. For most, it's a way to avoid loneliness, feel validation, and hide from problems. For the majority, it's a result of being pervasively influenced by a society that identifies premarital sex as the norm.

Premarital Sex Disclaimer

When someone asks women and girls of the consequences of premarital sex, they always give the same two answers: unwanted pregnancies and sexually transmitted diseases (STDs). Allow me to expose what Satan hides so well. These next two chapters will open your eyes to the many consequences of premarital sex that exceed beyond unwanted pregnancies and STDs. Have you ever been to a gym, enrolled children in a daycare center, or had to have a medical operation done whereby they provided you with all the risks that are possible as a result of their services to you? A *disclaimer* is a statement that reveals all the information and risks that are possible when you partake of something that the organization or person offers.

For example, some gyms may require you to sign a disclaimer where you agree that they are not responsible for any personal injury, accident, illness, or property damage that may occur during your use of their equipment and that you are fully aware of all possible risks. By signing the *disclaimer* statement, the person agrees to take on the risks and suffer any consequences that may occur as part of their participation. This person agrees that they will be on their own if something goes wrong and agrees that the gym is not held responsible.

This is what I tell women and girls: When you agree to have premarital sex, you sign an invisible disclaimer that states all the risks and consequences that result from having sex. You see, I had no manual when I was a teenager. Like many women and teenagers today, I was not aware of all the hidden truths behind sex. I wish someone had thought of a sex disclaimer before I started having sex at such an early age. You are blessed Ms. Diva because a while ago, God gave me this sex disclaimer metaphor so that I may share with you and the millions of other women and girls that He cares for so dearly. Below, I will provide you with my disclaimer for sexual intercourse so that you will be aware of all consequences and risks.

If you fully read your sex disclaimer before signing on for premarital sex (also known as fornication), it could save you from a lot of heartache, diseases, illnesses, setbacks, and more.

You've probably heard the familiar phrase that closed mouths don't get fed. Sometimes, men say things to women that imply that closed legs don't get fed when they try to get a female to have sex with them. They are implying that if you don't open your legs and give them sex, you won't reap the benefits that they have to offer and they will probably no longer want to give you their time. These days, even women reference the effects of getting "cobwebs" between their legs and tease that other women are angry and depressed because they haven't had sex in such a long time. In other words, "Closed legs don't get fed".

Well, in the next few pages, I'm here to confirm that men and women are right about something: "Closed legs **don't** get fed", but quite contrary to the way that it is normally conveyed. I want you to look at this "closed legs" thing a little differently.

From now on, remember the following:

Closed legs don't get fed uncontrolled emotions, absent baby fathers, sexual soul ties, abusive relationships, deferred dreams, decrease in dignity, unexpected pregnancies, or STDs.

Therefore, by keeping your legs closed (until marriage), you can save yourself from a lot of heartache, disappointments, and setbacks. This does not just apply to teenagers, but adult women as well. When we're in our twenties and thirties or older, we feel like the rules don't apply to us anymore. You see, sex before marriage (also known as premarital sex) can slow down a lot of dreams, blessings, and goals for you because not only is it a sin, but it feeds you so many unhealthy things.

> *With that said, here is your premarital sex disclaimer:*
>
> You are fully aware that engaging in premarital sex can result in uncontrolled emotions, absent baby fathers, sexual soul ties, abusive relationships, deferred dreams, a decrease in dignity, unexpected pregnancies, and STDs. When you consent to have sex, you agree to risk it all. You further agree that your sex partner will not be held responsible for any of these damages that you may encounter.

Diva to Diva

ℱ&

Like every other girl, the first time I engaged in premarital sex, I became an entirely different person. It changed my character, my outlook on life, shifted my focus, and caused many unstable emotions within me. The guy and I had daily conversations for almost a year, but I would never agree to date him. Finally, after he and his girlfriend broke up, I figured that since he had tried so hard and so long to get with me, that he really wanted me and was not worried about any other girl. What a common, foolish mistake young girls make! What a mistake that many women still make as adults! Needless to say, he continued to fool around with his former girlfriend! Shortly after having sex with him, he began ignoring some of my phone calls which tore me up on the inside. I felt rejected, used, and useless. I felt like he owed me something because he had been inside of me. I gave him a very valuable piece of me. This meant we should be together. This meant we would become closer. After all, giving him what he wanted made me special.

Wrong. Wrong. Wrong!

I started losing sleep immediately after having sex with him because all I thought about was this boy and how I had just had sex for the first time in my life. My thoughts and emotions literally consumed me! My grades started dropping in school because something else had taken precedence in my life. Now, this boy and my new sex life had become the priority. The thing is you can say that you won't allow it to interfere with your success, but the fact is— it does and oftentimes, it cannot be controlled.

After seeing the guy that I lost my virginity to at a school basketball game with his ex-girlfriend, I was livid! First, he stopped returning my phone calls and ignored me when I saw him. Then, I saw him hugged up with this girl at the game. The girl and I almost got in to a fight over this guy. Things escalated at school between the other girl and me. My grades dropped even lower. I lost even more sleep due to hurt and resentment. I know for a fact that I would not have been hurt as much if I had not given my body to him.

If I hadn't given my body to him, I would not have had anything to lose. He didn't have my heart because I wasn't in love with him. So, I would've left with everything I came in with— including my dignity. The guy gained bragging rights to his friends, but I suffered losses. What a waste, right? One little decision affected so much in my life. I felt humiliated because I was so stupid to give up my very valuable body part to someone who I would not even date in the future because he didn't belong in my destiny— someone who would not even matter to my future success.

౷

If I had read the sex disclaimer, it would have informed me that this guy did not owe me anything. I was the one who signed up for sex with him. He didn't force me.

When I signed up for premarital sex, I *unknowingly* signed a premarital sex disclaimer which stated that closed legs don't get fed uncontrolled emotions, depression, humiliation, and a decrease in my school achievements. I was responsible. I made the mistake. I had to suffer the consequences.

My disclaimer statement included all of these warnings, but I was just unaware of it! Please Ms. Diva, read your premarital sex disclaimer statement before consenting to sex. For those who are already engaged in sexual relationships, you should still read your sex disclaimer statement before consenting to have pre-marital sex again. It's not too late! Even for adult women!

Many women and girls get upset and frustrated at the guy because he cheated on her; he got her pregnant and refuses to take care of the baby; or he emotionally abused her. However, they signed on for these risks when they signed up for premarital sex. *They agreed to take the risks, suffer the possible consequences, and release the other partner of all responsibility.* The truth is those are some of the consequences of premarital sex. God is holy and our sins cannot go unpunished. A guy wants what he wants and your sex alone won't change his desires for other things and other women. Chances are: If you don't have his heart, you're not the only one in his shopping cart. If he's shopping around, why freely give up your prized possession? Sexual relations cause a woman to feel like the man owes her something. The guy owes you some of his time, energy, love, etc. After all, he was just inside of you and had taken a piece of your most intimate and valuable body part. This is what sends girls and women into an emotional prison. What you have between your legs does not secure your relationship with a guy. It doesn't matter what type of exotic things you can do with your body or how much he loves having sex with you. Just because he loves having sex with you doesn't mean you are the one he wants to spend his life with. Yes, you may be gorgeous with a beautiful body. But that body is not yours. It's God's body until you are married; then, it becomes your husband's body.

The Shackles of Sex

Premarital sex is yet another stronghold that keeps us chained as women in this society. What we think is so beneficial to us actually harms us. We continue to run back to the same things because Satan blinds us with temporary pleasures, worldly lusts, materialistic things, and popularity appeal. He blinds us from the truth so well that we never even realize that the very thing we keep doing is the core cause of so much chaos in our lives. The devil (your biggest enemy) is smart, very sneaky, and skilled in what he does.

Satan's trickery and craftiness are made evident here:

> I discovered that the things that were supposed to bring me life actually brought spiritual death to me. Sin took advantage of me and deceived me. It took the very thing that promised me life, pleasure, and happiness, and used it to destroy me. The very thing that I thought liberated me actually incarcerated me. It kept me in chains. Could it be that the good thing brought death to me? Absolutely not—because the "good thing" was actually never good. It just appeared to be good for me, but it was destruction all along. Sometimes, I do not understand my own actions or why I continue such behavior. Even when I want to do the right thing and change my ways, I find myself not being able to because the wrong things are always near and always available (Romans 7:10-25 Paraphrased).

Satan makes us think there is nothing wrong with premarital sex. Women think if they are truly in love, then that love should be shared through sex. Others think you don't have to be in love to have sex because it's just "casual" sex; there's nothing serious about it because they are not looking for a relationship with the guy; just sex.

The devil is so cunning! Satan leads women and girls to desire premarital sex and glorify it.

I see women discussing their sex lives all on social networks. Not only is she disrespecting God and her body through premarital sex, she's damaging her soul and doesn't even know it.

They do not realize that they have become a prisoner of Satan's tricks.

It is a weapon he uses to constantly destroy women and their destinies. Satan deceives them into believing that the best thing that they have going for themselves is sex so they keep going back to it. Many times, they expect something in return from the men which spirals into a cycle of hurt, rejection, and discouragement.

Then, there are women who have been hurt and scorn so many times that they are dead to these emotions. Additionally, in order to secure themselves from hurt and rejection, some women stop expecting anything from the men, except sex. This is settling, to say the least, and only sets them up for more failure. She may or may not be hurt from the man, but the premarital sex still takes a piece of her soul each time.

She may not experience emotional damage, but the *soul-damage* is inescapable!

These women are constantly "stuck" in a cycle!

They are stuck in bad relationships, financial distress, trouble with their children, job distress, etc.

Every time they take one step forward, they get knocked back four steps. They finally get on their feet, receive a new job, nice working car, and a little savings in their bank account. The next thing they know, they get into a car accident or their car breaks down, something gets stolen, or they lose the little money they had, and are now borrowing from Patricia to pay Pam.

Our women and girls are getting further and further away from the truth. Society says casual sex is the way of the world because times have changed and that's just how it is.

Let me stress to you that even though the world is constantly changing, God's word will *never* change. It clearly tells us that sexual immorality is a sin and He must punish us for fornication and adultery (1 Thessalonians 4:3-8 NIV).

Some of the chaos going on in women's lives today are the direct consequences of fornication or some other sins. Nevertheless, Satan deceives us into believing that fornication is not that big of a deal.

People have stopped discussing fornication as a sin.

The days are nearly extinct when people (saved as well as unsaved) encourage abstinence. Now, they only encourage our women and girls to "wrap it up"!

Such a smart and cunning way for Satan to conceal the truth which is that fornication is one of the most convincing demons that keep our women and girls in shackles.

The ugly truth is that sexual sin promises to fulfill our desires, but the reality is that it actually enlarges our desires.

> *"Hell and destruction are never full; so the eyes of a man [and woman] are never satisfied" (Proverbs 27:20).*

The more unholy sex we engage in, the more we want—the more we need—the more people we will affect—the more things we will lose in order to meet those desires. In short, the more sexual sin we commit, the more sin our flesh desires. Soon, Satan has such a stronghold on us until we are in too deep that we are in darkness to our own shackles.

Sex, Heart and Spirit

Now, understand this: I am in no way saying that you cannot be in a relationship based on true love. Honestly, I believe that there is truth in love at first sight because sometimes, God will place that feeling in your spirit. In fact, my husband and I experienced love at first sight at a very young age and it has proven true until today. Yes, true love relationships do still exist; in adults as well as teenagers. The heart is a very tricky thing Ms. Diva. The Bible says, *"The heart is deceitful above all things and beyond cure. Who can understand it"* (Jeremiah 17:9 NIV)? Sometimes, the heart is incapable of seeing things clearly. The heart seeks whatever is pleasing. The heart promises pleasure regardless of the truth; regardless of what's righteous. If being loved by a guy is what's pleasant to your heart, that's what the heart will promise to you; therefore, that's what you will believe whether it be true or false. You will then do whatever it takes to seek the pleasure that the heart has promised without realizing how your heart has deceived you. God instructs us to listen to what's within our spirit because the spirit knows the truth (See John 14:17). Always search your spirit or your *inner being;* trust your spirit over your heart. A little later, I will talk more about how you are still susceptible to all of the consequences of sex even if the guy *is* your soul mate. True love is an element of marriage; it is not a replacement for marriage. Just because a guy and a woman are in true love does not excuse her from the consequences of premarital sex.

I was always very wise for a girl my age.

Yet, my life events prove that I wasn't exempt.

You are not exempt!

No one is exempt from the emotional pain that premarital sex causes. Emotional pain is a major consequence of sexual intercourse. When sexual intercourse becomes a factor, emotions almost always become affected. I am in no way telling you that sex is an awful thing. Quite the contrary! Sex was designed by God as a remarkably amazing connection between a husband and a wife. People today look at sex as something to do just for fun. It's just leisure to many people. However, look at it this way: Suppose you think bungee jumping looks fun, but when it's time for you to try it, they tell you the rope is loose and will probably break. Just because you think bungee jumping looks fun, causes you to look cool, and feels good, does that mean you should risk your life and future to experience temporary pleasure? People take hundreds of risks each time they engage in premarital sex.

Sexual Soul Ties

A soul tie is when your soul is knitted together with another soul to become one soul. When you have sex with anyone (whether you're married or unmarried), you create a sexual soul tie with that person. Many women and girls think, "Oh, he didn't mean anything to me. We just had sex." God makes it clear that sex is so serious and special that it doesn't matter *who* we have sex with. Whether he's bum status or boss status, sexual intercourse makes you *one* with that person (1 Corinthians 6:16). Married couples have a *positive* and *productive*

Sex during marriage is the only type of unchained sex because instead of being punished by God, you will be blessed by God .

soul tie. When you fornicate or engage in premarital sex, you develop a *negative* and *destructive* soul tie with that person. Have you ever seen a woman who gets beaten by her boyfriend continue to run back to the abusive man even after she has been freed? Do you know that woman or girl whose boyfriend constantly cheats on her and although she knows it's not wise of her, she continues to give him chance after chance?

She continues to put up with his infidelity over and over. She continues to accept his lies time after time; disrespect after disrespect; humiliation after humiliation. Most likely, these women don't even know why they keep running back to men who abuse, misuse, and disrespect them. They don't understand why they continue to place themselves in positions to be hurt repeatedly. But God knows why and so does Satan. Satan knows because he has wrapped chains around our women and girls and developed a stronghold in their minds so that they can keep running back to the very thing that is destroying them: the shackles of premarital sex. The woman keeps going back because she's trying to fill the void; the emptiness of her soul that she gave up to him during sex. Not only has the man taken a piece of her soul, but she is also walking around with a piece of his soul. It is frustrating, to say the least, to walk around with someone else's demons and spir-

Sexual sins give Satan permission to attach his demons to you through the tunnel of soul ties.

its. You don't understand yourself sometimes or why you do certain things because another person's soul has the power over you. And more than likely, you are totally clueless to the skeletons in his closets—the demons of his past. Therefore, there is no way to understand the turmoil that's going on inside of you because it came from him, but is now a part of you.

There's no way to understand his soul because he was not designed to be your husband. There's no way to understand the demons this guy struggles with; which you are now dealing with as well.

I pray the Holy Spirit helps you grasp this!

You don't just transfer orgasms, vaginal secretions, and semen; you transfer souls when you have sex. Period. Therefore, you don't know why you do the things you do. It's called strongholds. You see, sexual sins give Satan permission to attach his demons to you through the tunnel of soul ties.

Some women don't return to the same guy, but go and engage in premarital sex with another guy—still to fill the same void from premarital sex with a previous guy.

Can you imagine how spiritually frustrating it is for a woman who has slept with several men? She now walks around with the inadequacies, attitudes, emotions, and spirits of not one, but numerous other souls.

How can a woman or girl remain focused on her destiny when she is polluted with all these inner issues?

How can a woman or girl be available for the husband God has created for her when her soul is so occupied with the souls of other men?

My soul and spirit were penetrated because this guy that I lost my virginity to had now become a small part of me that I didn't know how to take back. My soul had connected with his soul which was not the soul that God had designed for me. When you allow all other different kinds of souls and spirits to enter your body, it is confusion at its best. Why?

All of a sudden, you are no longer content in your soul because another soul different than yours and different than that of your soul-mate has entered your precious, blood-bought body. Soon, you find yourself continuously returning to sex with the same guy or different guys in order to ease frustration or to fill the void within you. All along, you are unaware that the reason you feel so much void and frustration is because that guy was not your soul mate. Your heart has deceived you. Moreover, the void is a result of sexual sins. In the next chapter, I will discuss more of how God showed me the way that sexual sins impacted my soul and almost destroyed me. I want you to know that there is hope for those engaged in sexual sins. You do not have to walk around with soul ties. God forgives and His power breaks the chains of sexual impurity. The Bible tells us that if we disengage ourselves from the sexual sins and unite ourselves with God, we become one spirit with God (1 Corinthians 6:18). Seek God to fill your void and verbally renounce all sexual soul ties with those you have had sex with. Chapter four will help guide you through this, if needed.

SEX: *Body, Soul, & Spirit*

I know what society has taught us. I know that Satan has deceived us into believing that abstaining until marriage is a thing of the past; that only old people and conservative people adhere to it. I refuse to let my sisters continue to live such a lie, a lie that causes destruction and delays in one's destiny. Abstaining until one is married was not designed by the government, old people, or conservative Christians. Sex was orchestrated by God. He clearly states that sex is designed to be saved for marriage (1 Corinthians 7:2). Whether you're fourteen or forty years old, sex outside of marriage is a sin—period! Premarital sex wounds the soul and hinders progress—period!

God did not make this a rule in order to be cruel. The reason God wants you to refrain from sexual sin is because it wars against your soul (1 Peter 2:11).

He made this a commandment literally to protect us from all the life-long consequences of sex. Abstaining from sex until marriage is God's way of protecting your body, soul, and spirit. Sex is an amazing, invigorating, and sensational phenomenon for married people *between a man and a woman.*

When we do things outside of God's will, that's when consequences happen. When a husband and wife come together for sex, the man enters the woman and their spirits/souls connect as one. When your spirit connects with someone, trust me: you want it to be with someone that you are committed to for life—your husband. Otherwise, you are creating a bond with someone else's soul. And this soul owes you no goodwill or commitment. Believe it or not, sexual intercourse is a spiritual thing far more than physical. Most women and girls get emotionally attached when having sex because it was designed to be a spiritual and emotional connection with your soul mate—the man God designed for you—the man whose rib you are.

The confusion, frustration, and curses come when you become one soul with someone other than your husband.

Your vagina, the most intimate part of your body gets penetrated during sex. Do you know what else gets penetrated during sex? Your soul and spirit.

It doesn't matter if you're 14 or 44, the impact to the soul and spirit will still occur. Your vagina is very sacred, which means it should be private, set apart, and only shared with your heaven-sent husband. "You were bought with a price, therefore glorify God with your bodies, and in your spirit, which are God's"(1 Corinthians 6:20). Your body is a temple of the Lord.

The way we honor him is by honoring our bodies that God has blessed us with and by not allowing unfamiliar spirits to enter our bodies, souls, or spirits.

Jesus shed His blood for that beautiful body of yours. It belongs to Him only—until you marry. Sex during marriage is the only type of unchained sex because instead of being punished by God, you will be blessed by God (Hebrews 13:4).

You are now knowledgeable of the things that you will *not* get fed by abstaining from premarital sex. You are aware that you are responsible for any consequences that you may endure as a result of premarital sex. I have written the sex disclaimer that I just discussed. If you are ready, please read it, sign it, and keep it for your reference. Try God in this area. You will see chains broken and blessings released in more ways than one.

Premarital Sex Disclaimer

by Dr. Nioka Smith|www.drniokasmith.com

Abstaining from sex until marriage is God's way of protecting your body, soul, and spirit. "Flee fornication. Every sin that a man does is without the body; but he that commits fornication *sins against his own body.*" 1 Cor. 6:18

I am fully aware that engaging in premarital sex can result in uncontrolled emotions, absent baby fathers, sexual soul ties, abusive relationships, deferred dreams, a decrease in dignity, unexpected pregnancies, or STDs. When I consent to have sex, I agree to risk it all. I further agree that no one else can be blamed for any suffering that I may endure as a result.

Acknowledged this _____ Day of _____ , 20 ___ .

Name _____

Signature _____

Dear Diva,
It would do my heart well if you would send a copy of your signed Sex Disclaimer to the business address or email address below. This is voluntary and may be used for data reports and other ministry purposes. If used, your first name will be concealed.
~Dr. Nioka

Dr. Nioka Smith Ministries
6104 Forbing Rd
Little Rock, AR 72209
Email: info@drniokasmith.com

4

Closed Legs Don't Get Fed

Part II: Recommitment

৵

When you have premarital sex with someone that God didn't design for you, your spirit man is troubled, creating war within your inner self. Why is this so? Your spirit or soul has just connected with another spirit or soul that wasn't created for you. I Corinthians 2:11 says, "After all, who knows everything about a person except that person's own spirit" (GWT)? If husband and wife are one, this means that they are one in the spirit as well. Simply put, their spirits are connected. Your spirit knows when a spirit different from yours has entered in. Your spirit (inner man) knows the spirit (inner man) of your God-designed husband. Problems arise when you go against this will of God and allow another guy—who is not your husband—to enter your body and soul. In order to fulfill the void and the confusion caused by broken hearts, most women and girls have sex with another man because they are vulnerable. When you are vulnerable or weak, you oftentimes fall into traps. Let's discuss the trap I fell in and how premarital sex caused my spirit man to be troubled; thus, creating a war within my inner self.

Diva to Diva

At the beginning of my senior year of high school, I was an honor student in the top five of my class of approximately two hundred students. I had a cumulative GPA of a 3.9 and was enrolled in several advanced courses. I was voted most popular and Vice President of my senior class, had a part time job, and was searching for colleges and scholarships. I was close friends with the entire crew of the most popular girls in my class. On top of all of this, my relationship with the love of my life was perfect! Life as I knew it could not have been greater! Until…

My relationship with the long time love of my life became rocky and distant. Coral (or Rell, as I so affectionately call him) and I had broken up several times before, but nothing like this final break-up!

Out of despair from our breakup, I fell into one of Satan's traps. I was so weak and vulnerable at this time that I just wanted to feel better from my heartbreak with Rell. After all, he was my longtime boyfriend and the love of my life.

I decided to hang out with some friends over a classmate's house and out of despair, I ended up having sex with a friend. Terrence was a really close friend of mine.

We had a history of talking over the phone helping each other through different problems. He would cry to me over the phone or in person about the pain of missing his mother and I would share things with him. I absolutely had no feelings for him in a boyfriend/girlfriend kind of way. I cared for him and loved him as a friend, but nothing more.

One evening, a few friends (male and female) decided to all spend the night over Terrence's house. He lived with his aunt and uncle, but had a bedroom on a separate side of their house. Therefore, the adults weren't aware that there was a slumber party going on.

So, I spent the night over Terrence's house to "kick it" as friends like usual. We laughed, joked around, and talked about everything and nothing at the same time.

Before I knew it, Terrence was caressing me and kissing me.

Everything in my head said to stop him.

Everything in my head said don't let him take it there Nioka; you two are friends. But everything in my heart said I needed this and that it would help me feel better. The anguish in my heart said this would help compensate for the pain and emptiness I felt from my break up with Rell.

After it was all over, I felt worse than I did before.

I felt more emptiness.

I didn't know then that our hearts can deceive us based on our emotions. I didn't know that connecting with another soul through the acts of sexual sin only takes more pieces of our soul away.

I felt worse and emptier because I kept looking for something to fill my void—never realizing that sin is the hungriest predator alive and its belly is never full.

After a couple of months, Rell and I were still not speaking to each other. In my mind and heart, I just knew it was officially over between us. I was so distraught. He was the love of my life! Usually, our arguments always brought us back around in a couple of days. This time, it was different. We were broken up for real.

One day, it occurred to me that I had not had my menstrual cycle in over two months. I didn't think anything of it because I had recently been on birth control and I rarely came on my period. However, as the time passed by and I still hadn't come on my menstrual cycle, I decided to go to Wal-Mart to buy two pregnancy tests. I took one test that night and the result was positive. I called a friend in tears informing her that the test showed that I was pregnant. We were both in doubt. I said surely this test is wrong. I took the second test in the morning and it was positive as well. I did not believe I was pregnant. Besides, I had stopped having sex the past couple of months and made up my mind to abstain from sex and focus on my education and my relationship with God.

This could not be true, I hoped.

After denying that the results were true, I went to the health department to keep it a secret from my parents. I remember the nurse's words so clearly. It felt like she spoke in very slow motion. I felt like I was in a horror movie with time slowing down. In my eyes, her lips were moving very slowly. Her eyes were moving in slow motion, and so were her hand gestures.

Slowly, I heard these words,

"Well, the other tests you took were accurate.

You are pregnant, sweetie."

After this, she kept talking for a while but I cannot tell you one bit of what she said. It was all distorted. I remember getting up and walking out without saying a word.

She followed behind me and said, "Sweetie, I can help you. You have options. What are you going to do? Are you going to keep the baby?"

"Keep the baby?" I thought. "What baby? I can't have a baby. I'm only 17 years old. I'm going to college next year. If I go through with this, I won't be able to go to college; let alone a reputable college. All my dreams will go down the drain."

So, at this moment, I started to realize that this thing may just be real. But I was still in just a little bit of denial. I didn't think this would happen to me. I said, "What do they know? I'm going to a real doctor!"

I went to the doctor's office and the doctor spoke these exact words..."Ms. Taylor, you are pregnant."

That was it.

I was pregnant. Within about six months, I would go from teenager to mother.

The teen pregnancy rate is approximately four out of ten girls[1] and within a blink of an eye, I was a part of those numbers. Just when I had decided to become abstinent, I found out I was becoming a statistic.

When the storms blow, they roar! Not only was I seventeen and pregnant, but I had to find out if the father of my baby was Rell (my ex-boyfriend/the love of my life) or Terrence (a good friend that I had sex with out of heartache).

This was indeed the ultimate Maury Povich scenario!

I was so humiliated because of this. I was not promiscuous at all! I was not a girl that "slept around".

I thought to myself,

"Out of all people, how could this happen to me?"

There I was with the possibility that this other guy, Terrence could be my baby's father. This was a guy and a friend that I had sex with out of emotional pain and vulnerability and was never even in a relationship with!

This was supposed to happen to promiscuous girls only, not me!

Since it had been almost three months since I had sex, I attempted to figure out the calculations based on what I read on pregnancies. I knew that Terrence was the last person I had sex with. I remembered the date so well because the day I spent the night over Terrence's house—the day I first had sex with him, was my late grandfather's birthday. The truth is that before our break-up, Rell and I had sex so often that I couldn't remember those dates. There were countless times with Rell. However, I

Just when I had decided to become abstinent, I found out I was becoming a statistic.

knew for sure that Rell and I had broken up before Terrence and I had sex. I also knew for a fact that when I was with Rell, he was the only one I was having sex with. And after our big breakup, Terrence was the only person I was having sex with. So, I used the calculation method and the dates added up to be Terrence's baby. After a few days of getting myself together, I called Terrence to tell him that I needed to pick him up so we could drive somewhere and talk. I told him that I was pregnant by him. He told me had a feeling that's what I was about to tell him. After a conversation about him promising to "have my back" and calling his brother to share the news, this led to more ongoing sex with Terrence throughout my pregnancy. Countless times, I snuck out of my mother's house in the wee hours of the night to go spend the night at his house. It didn't even resonate with me that we were just teenage children in high school. On school nights, we slept together in his bed and woke up the next morning right before it was time for the both of us to get ready for school.

Most of the times, he called for me. But sometimes when I was emotional or feeling distraught, I would call him to let him know I was on my way over his house. Even though we weren't in a relationship, I didn't want to feel the pain that I was feeling at home, so I kept having sex with Terrence because I had given Satan permission to chain me with a sexual stronghold. This nonstop unprotected sex with Terrence led to me contracting two sexually transmitted diseases (STDs). After one of my pre-natal check-ups at the doctor's office, I received a phone call saying that I had Chlamydia and Gonorrhea. Terrence was the only guy that I was having sex with and he burned me with not one, but two STDs while I was pregnant!

$$\mathcal{S}$$

The Blindfolds of Sexual Sin

How in the world did my life get here? I couldn't say I had hit rock bottom because the truth is I felt like I was in a never ending pit with no bottom. When was it going to end? It was blow after blow—all as a result of being outside of God's will. As if being a statistic of teen pregnancy wasn't enough, I had now become a statistic of sexually transmitted diseases. I was so disgusted—mainly with myself. When I went to Terrence's house to tell him that he "burned" me with two diseases, he in-formed me that he felt like he had some kind of disease because he wasn't "peeing right". He said that he had just recently gone to the doctor and received medication for it. He showed me his pill bottles and apologized for infecting me as he pulled me to the bed in an attempt to console me. Needless to say, I was inconsolable. I was seventeen, pregnant, and infected.

It's crazy how the deceit of sexual sin targets our heart and our emotions.

My heart was aching so badly from falling out with Rell. My acts of sexual sin with Rell led to the vulnerability from our breakup, which led to the ongoing sex relationship with Terrence, which led to the STDs, which then led to an amplified emotional rollercoaster. My emotions were all over the place ranging from emptiness and disappointments to humiliation, heartbreak, and desolation. On top of that, I was deeply wounded from abuse and violence within my home (to be discussed in a later chapter). Talking to Terrence all night as we shared each other's pain, emotions, and tears about his late mother and my family, discussing baby names with Terrence, bonding with each other, spending the nights with him, and having ongoing sex with him—was all supposed to ease my pain and fill my void. However, it only created more void and emptiness within me. For the life of me, I couldn't understand why I felt so empty.

❧

I felt worse and emptier because I kept looking for something to fill my void—never realizing that sin is the hungriest predator alive and its belly is never full.

It was because my soul was in search for wholeness and the enemy deceived me into thinking that I could fill the void with sex.

However, sin cannot provide wholeness.

Wholeness is found only in God.

Yet, I was a pregnant teenage girl with raging hormones and unstable emotions who kept going back to sexual sin because my soul was crying out.

I didn't realize that every time you return to the sexual sin, instead of soothing your soul, it takes even more of your soul.

If I was as spiritually mature as I am today, I would've been cognizant of the destructive seeds that Satan plants in your life when you engage in premarital sex.

Satan's advantage over you is that these sexual strongholds are not tangible. You can't see or feel the demonic strongholds attaching themselves to you because they are spirits. The sexual strongholds may not be tangible, but they are just as real as the person who sits next to you at any given moment.

Here's how Satan works against what you cannot see with your natural eyes or feel with your natural hands.

> When an evil spirit leaves a person, it goes into the desert, seeking rest but finding none. This it says, 'I will return to the person I came from. 'So it returns and finds its former home empty, swept, and in order. Then the spirit finds seven other spirits more evil than itself, and they all enter the person and live there. And so that person is worse off than before. That will be the experience of this evil generation.
> (Matthew 12:43-45 NLT)

We can also view these evil spirits as destructive seeds that are planted in us as a result of sexual sins. They attach themselves to you without you feeling or seeing them. Next thing you know, you find yourself asking:
"Why do I keep going back to the same guy that I know is no good for me?
"When did I start crying all the time?
"How do I keep ending up in the same place with men? In my career?
"How come every time I think I'm progressing in life, I get knocked back?"

Don't be fooled. Sexual sins cause you to reap consequences beyond your relationships. God wants me to tell you that sexual sins promise you abundant fulfillment, but breeds perpetual emptiness. The deceit in it all is that Satan wants you to believe that the consequences are limited to unexpected pregnancies and STDs because those are things that are tangible. You can see and feel a pregnancy. You can see and feel the side effects of an STD, but you cannot see or feel those sexual demons that have multiplied and become stronger than before! The more you engage in sexual sins, the more those demons multiply and the more powerful they become so that every time you try to walk away, strongholds confine you.

Sexual sins promise you abundant fulfillment, but breeds perpetual emptiness.

The more I engaged in continual premarital sex with Terrence, the more the sexual spirits multiplied, exacerbated, and spiraled out of control (see Matthew 12:43-45). God wants you to break from the chains of sexual strongholds as well. Whether you are an adult woman or a teenage girl, God wants you to know the truth so that it may indeed set you free. Sadly, I knew that Terrence had a girlfriend out of town. It was fine with me that he slept with other girls around town that I knew about— even ones that he told me about. I was okay with the fact that he and I were not in a boyfriend/girlfriend relationship. I was okay with our "friends with benefits" package because initially, I didn't think there was much harm in casual sex.

I lowered my dignity and accepted it all because I felt so vulnerable and full of void. Because not only was I experiencing guilt and disappointment from my pregnancy and heartbreak from the breakup with Rell, but I was also experiencing a lot of pain from domestic violence at home. So, I gave my soul to someone who wasn't designed for me. I was so frustrated in my spirit. I felt so lost.

So disconnected from who I was. So empty.

I felt in a world by myself. I didn't understand what was going on with me. The new life growing inside of me had completely taken over my body and emotions. I never thought I'd be that girl. You know, the one who doesn't care if she's the *other* woman. The one who only wants to have "casual" sex with a guy. The one who has a baby as a result of a one night stand. The one who has a baby by a guy that she is not even in a relationship with. The one who allows a guy to infect her with STDs, knowing that he was promiscuous.

The thing is I didn't care.

I didn't care about myself.

I didn't care about school.

I didn't care about life.

I knew there was a deep hole in my heart; but at the time, I didn't know there was a hole in my soul too—a hole that was being filled by darkness (also known as sexual soul ties and strongholds). I grew further and further away from God, which was actually the only thing that would fill my void from the invasion of the sexual soul ties and strongholds.

This book is heavily inspired by II Corinthians 10:4:

"For the weapons of our warfare are not carnal, but mighty through God, to the pulling down of strongholds."

The seventeen year old Nioka didn't know that in order to fight for our souls and spiritual freedom, we must use the spiritual power of God. The only way to see spiritually is to use spiritual eyes.

If you're willing and ready to take off the spiritual blindfolds, turn the page and say the prayer.

Dear Lord,
I ask for your forgiveness in the sins I have committed knowingly and unknowingly. I ask that you would open my spiritual eyes and reveal to me the way Satan has deceived my mind concerning sex. I pray that you would shift my desires in a way that pleases you. Teach me how to examine my life concerning sexual sins and grant me the power to overcome them. .
In Jesus' name, Amen.

From Choices to Consequences

I was no longer a part of the "most popular pretty girl" clique. After it was revealed that I was *allegedly* carrying Terrence's baby, I lost my closest friends. They stopped hanging with me and even began walking on eggshells when I came around. I was fed *rejection* at this point. I told Terrence I wanted a paternity test, but rumors spread that he was the one who requested it because he didn't know if the baby was his. This was very far from the truth and the rumors caused more stress on me and my pregnancy. I was hospitalized twice for going into preterm labor. Fortunately, they were able to stop my labor both times so that I would not have a premature baby. While I'm sure Terrence may have had some reservations about the paternity from time to time, he never once approached me about a paternity test. When I went to him expressing *my* desire to have one, he agreed. After I contracted the STDs at seven months pregnant, Terrence and I began to talk less and less each day. Because Terrence and I were two of the most popular students in the twelfth grade, *everybody* was in our business and secretly praying that it was not his baby that I was carrying. The truth is that while they were praying against it, I felt hopeless and depressed at the thought of having a baby by my friend Terrence. I wasn't hopeless and depressed because he was some awful guy. Despite the repulsive STDs he infected me with, he was a really great person and dear friend. We've always had high respect for each other even unto this day. But when I started thinking about the next eighteen years, I felt like I had cheated myself out of the family and life that I always envisioned for myself.

I feared a broken family for my child.

I thought about the struggles of a single-parent lifestyle for myself. Even at the age of seventeen, I knew I didn't want this. I needed someone who would not just be financially present, but emotionally, spiritually, and physically present as well.

I needed someone who would show my son how to cherish a woman by the way he treated me.

So I felt hopeless because I could not see this life as being possible with Terrence.

The truth is it depressed me to know that I'd be that girl with a "baby daddy". Because although Terrence was a great person and loving friend, his loyalty toward a friend and his loyalty toward a girlfriend were on two opposite ends of the commitment spectrum. Terrence's rampant sexual reputation of his overwhelming need to sleep with multiple women was a lifestyle that I would never have accepted in normal circumstances. It was a lifestyle that I did not want for my child, even if Terrence and I were only co-parenting.

Nonetheless, Terrence didn't force me to accept his lifestyle and he didn't lie about it.

By signing on to a sexual relationship with him, I accepted the risk of possibly having to live with his lifestyle for at least eighteen years.

As stated in my sex disclaimer, when we agree to have sex, we are aware of all of the consequences and no one can be blamed for any suffering that we endure.

The fact is that I consented to every sexual occurrence with Terrence, being well aware of his reputation and sexual behavior. I signed the sex disclaimer by consenting to premarital sex; therefore, I was held accountable for the consequences.

So while other girls chatted about how juicy this gossip was, I felt like I had lost.

I felt like I had lost out on a life with my soulmate. I felt I had lost the chance at my "forever after" with the man who would treat me like a queen, cherish me, protect and provide for me, would be committed to *only* me, and would raise our family with Godly principles.

That someone was Rell. Terrence and I were close friends who had love for each other, but we were never in a relationship. Rell, on the other hand, was the guy that still gave me butterflies long after our breakup.

Most women and girls don't think this way, but I wanted a *family* for my son. I wanted what was most beneficial for my son.

Even in all my shortcomings as an emotionally-wrecked teen, I knew there was a difference between a *present* father and an *active* father.

~

1 out of every 4 children are being raised without a father [2] and nearly half live below the poverty line. [3]

After nine months of pain and agony, the paternity tests showed that Terrence was *not* my child's father. Rell, whom I was in love with—the one that I had broken up with, the one that I had wished the entire pregnancy to be my child's father—was actually my child's father. After all this time, it turned out that I was wrong all along. Or as I deeply believe, it turns out that God took my mess and made a miracle out of it. He worked it out in my favor. Although I was extremely relieved and grateful to know that my soul mate, Rell had fathered my baby instead of Terrence, I also felt *horrible* to have led Terrence astray into believing that I was carrying his baby.

So now, in the midst of all of my happiness that Rell was my baby's father, my shame and guilt lingered for a long while.

Having contracted two STDs from Terrence, becoming a pregnant teen, plummeting in my academics, experiencing the pain from the belief that it was not my boyfriend's baby, feeling like an outcast, suffering isolation and humiliation, and all the crucial family issues that I dealt with at home—was more than enough to bear for a seventeen year old senior high school student.

The rumors didn't help, of course. All kinds of rumors circulated that I was after his money. However, Terrence knew me better than that and understood that I was not a gold-digger like many other shallow-minded girls. He knew I didn't want his money and I witnessed as he made it clear to his brother and family that I was not *that kind of girl.*

In fact, after I found out that the baby wasn't his, I calculated all the hundreds of dollars that he and his family had given me, used my savings from the summer, and wrote a money order for the same amount to reimburse them even after Terrence insisted that I didn't pay them back.

I knew inside of me that I would be every bit of prosperous within a moment's time, so I wasn't concerned about money.

Temporary money never intrigued me—but, long term prosperity always has.

On the other hand, I was exceedingly overjoyed that my soul mate ended up being the father of my child. I was grateful for the mercy of not having to deal with a split family after all.

However, like any other teen mom, I still had consequences to deal with, such as the painful remnants of my senior high school year and the years it took to recover from the humiliation, disappointment, lack of dignity, depression and guilt, etc.

~

You see, even though the baby seemed to have brought my boyfriend, Rell and I back together, I still encountered so much turmoil because of my decisions. The choices you make today dramatically affect tomorrow. Even if you are madly in love and the guy is truly in love with you, emotional pain still occurs anytime you have premarital sex with someone. Emotional pain is a consequence of premarital sex. Period! Rell and I were in true love. It was one hundred percent real! In fact, we are very happily married today. However, because we were having premarital sex (fornication), we had to suffer overwhelming consequences.

Again, I say to you:

Closed legs don't get fed uncontrolled emotions, absent baby fathers, sexual soul ties, abusive relationships, deferred dreams, decrease in dignity, unexpected pregnancies, or STDs.

I did not keep my legs closed and I was fed *almost* all of the above consequences just from having premarital sex. I was fed two sexually transmitted diseases from a *different* guy (Terrence). I was fed an unexpected pregnancy from my boyfriend although I did not know that it was Rell's baby at the time. I was fed depression because I was the talk of my town, and three other towns!

I was depressed because in *my* mind, I was carrying somebody's baby who I clearly would not be with because we were not in love with each other. I was depressed because in *my* mind, the father of my unborn child was not Rell. In *my* mind, my relationship with the love of my life was *over* because I had gotten myself pregnant by someone else. This was all before I knew that the baby was not Terrence's baby, but it was indeed Rell's baby.

I was fed uncontrolled emotions that totally consumed me. I pictured my college career going down the drain. I thought about having to have a part time baby's father. Other uncontrolled emotions resulted from how I assumed I was being perceived by my family. I was supposed to be the first one to receive a college degree. I was supposed to be the one who would get out of our impoverished hometown and make something out of myself. Now what was I supposed to do? How was I supposed to take care of a baby? How was I supposed to go to college now? My emotions were out of control which in turn brought a few suicidal thoughts into my mind. I'd sometimes get into my car and drive down a dark highway in the middle of the night secretly hoping someone would run into me.

I was fed a decrease in academics because the entire time that I was on homebound (schooling from home), I must've completed only five assignments in all of my classes combined. I was too depressed for school. Suddenly, so many other things took precedence over my school work. My grades dropped tremendously from all As to Cs.

I kept having sexual intercourse with Terrence on the regular even when we had stopped talking to each other at school.

I always refused to be this girl.

Yet, there I was, decreasing my dignity by the pounds and feeling more depressed by the minute that I had become somebody's "baby mama". I had turned into the biggest gossip of the school.

~

It's so crazy how your life can be a certain way one day and dramatically different the very next day all because of a choice that you made—that at the time, did not appear that it would have so many consequences. I was shunned by a lot of people because so many were appalled at 'Nioka' making such a "careless" and "unwise" choice. They all figured it did not fit my character to make such a "mistake". Their disappointment in me breathed so loudly.

All the places where I would normally fit in, I didn't fit anymore. I felt so alone!

All of the above led to me having so many uncontrolled emotions such as feelings of inadequacy, guilt, hurt, depression, etc. I was fed humiliation as a result of premarital sex because I was wrong about who my baby's father was! I never thought this could happen to me when I wasn't even promiscuous.

But that's one of the consequences that open legs get fed.

Everyone's story is different Ms. Diva. Another woman's deferred dreams, lack of dignity, humiliation, and uncontrolled emotions may look different from mine. However, the fact remains that premarital sex forces you to suffer consequences in ways far beyond that of unexpected pregnancies and sexually transmitted diseases.

There are more detrimental consequences than unexpected pregnancies, such as the agony of living with someone else's soul, years of spiritual frustration that causes you to stay in the same place in life, and the life-long financial struggles because the results of the decision that you made deferred your dreams, etc. Every choice leads to consequences that extends beyond your control and can last for decades.

Lastly, because I did not keep my legs closed, I was fed a lack of dignity. I had no self-control because my life was clearly out-of-control. I definitely did not feel a sense of self-worth. I stooped so low in my association with Terrence.

I became someone with very little standards.

I felt like my life was not going anywhere and that my life wasn't worth anything anymore. I felt like I didn't deserve anything in life. My dignity had been suppressed by all the darkness that I permitted in my soul as a result of sexual sin. Throughout this book, you will see that God gave me back my dignity coupled with prosperity. He wants to do the same for you.

What I want you to see, Ms. Diva, is that regardless of the situation; whether the guy only wants you for sex, deeply cares for you, or truly loves you, the fact is that pre-marital sex comes flooded with consequences. **The problems you suffer don't always stem from the guy; they stem from the sin.**

These consequences can happen whether you are promiscuous or not. I was not promiscuous at all. Even still, sexual sin is sexual sin.

Whether in love or not; promiscuous or not, consequences beyond our control will occur.

Don't ever make a decision without considering the long-term consequences. You must ask yourself what types of consequences come with the choice. If you ask yourself this question, it will save you from a lot of trouble and setbacks. The consequences of sexual sins come in different forms and at different times whether it is through STDs, emotional pain, humiliation, unexpected pregnancies, deferred dreams, decreased dignity, and more. Just because someone hasn't reaped their punishments yet doesn't mean their time is not coming.

Truth be told: most of them *are* reaping their consequences through the chaos that they are experiencing in their lives. However, they are blinded to the fact that it is a result of premarital sex. *Premarital sex plus love equal consequences. Premarital sex minus love equal consequences.* Love makes no difference in this situation.

Bodily Harm

What happened during the creation of man and woman was a spiritual connection. Society is getting farther and farther away from God's plan which is why more and more cases of STDs are occurring today. God is holy and must punish sin. Marriage is holy and the bed undefiled, but God will judge fornicators (Hebrews 13:4). Undefiled means clean.

On the other hand, the bed is defiled (contaminated, foul, or unclean) with premarital sex. It is because of this that all other physical consequences of pre-marital sex occur such as STDs. It is why I contracted *not one, but two* STDs. Thank God the STDs were cured and did not affect my baby! However, it very well could have affected my baby and I could have received an STD that was incurable.

Anytime you have premarital sex, you don't have the same covering/protection over you that married couples have because the bed (or place) that you have sex in is cursed. It is dirty. Contaminated. Defiled. Unfortunately, STDs are some of the dirty, contaminated, cursed consequences that come along with sexual sins.

Every time you have premarital sex, you are not only sinning against God; but guess what, you are also sinning against your own body.

That's right. The bible says, "Flee fornication, every sin that a man does is without the body, but whoever sins sexually, sins against their own body" (1 Corinthians 6:18).

When you have pre-marital sex, your body is the one *doing* the sin and your body is the object that the sin is being done *against*. This is why all the diseases are so prevalent today. It's everywhere because pre-marital sex is happening more and more today. The more that sexual sin occurs, the more cases of diseases occur.

STDs don't discriminate. Just as bullets have no eyes, STDs have no feelings. They don't care how young or old you are! They don't care how good of a person you are.

I never would have thought I'd be a victim of STDs; I never thought I'd be a teen mom. Chlamydia and gonorrhea didn't care that I was carrying life inside of me or that if I had waited any longer to get cured, my baby could have been born with long-term defects.

Chlamydia and gonorrhea couldn't empathize with me being just a child having a child. *The diseases simply attached themselves to my sinful act and invaded my soul and body-with the permission I gave them when I unknowingly signed the sex disclaimer.*

Sadly, we are getting further and further away from God's truth. Of course, sin has been existent since the fall of man; but even still, there once was a time (not long ago) when people regarded marriage and sex as more than just a pastime. The uncompromising truth is that sexually transmitted diseases are more prevalent in our world today because sexual sins are running rampant like never before. Regardless of race or age, the fact is that sexual sins cause weaknesses, diseases, and eventually shorten one's life in one way or another. Choose to be free, choose to be safe, and choose to be abstinent until marriage! Protect your own body.

The Three R's

If you are no longer a virgin, there is good news! God forgives and renews. If you are sexually active, make the choice today to recommit yourself to purity. You have heard that experience is the best teacher. May I stress that with some things, you do not need experience to teach you. You need to take heed to warning and advice. Please Ms. Diva, don't let experience lead you to destruction. Allowing experience to be your teacher when it comes to premarital sex is like playing Russian roulette with your future. You are taking a gamble on your precious life and soul. Please don't let experience be your teacher in this area.

Celibacy is when you have been sexually active, but have now decided to abstain from sex until marriage. Becoming celibate simply means recommitting your body back to God. He is able to restore your body, heart, and soul. He forgives us *immediately* when we repent and He no longer remembers our sins (Micah 7:19). God is that kind of God!

I regained my dignity, took back my power over my body and emotions, and took control over my life with what I call "*The Three R's*": Repent, Renounce, & Recommit.

Repent: *"Repent, then, and turn to God, so that your sins may be wiped out, that times of refreshing may come from the Lord"* *(Acts 3:19 NIV).*

When we repent, we approach God with remorse for our actions and ask for forgiveness with a set mind to change our behavior and turn away from our sins. Be sure to state the sexual sin (fornication) that you are repenting from. After I saw how far I had fallen from the will of God, I repented and I knew He had forgiven me immediately. We must be aware that temptations will definitely come (1 Corinthians 10:13). After I repented and had decided (again) to abstain from sex, multiple sexual temptations came by way of Terrence again. Long after I had given birth to my son and had found out the paternity, Terrence continued to pursue me. God tells us that being tempted is not a sin, but the sin is when we act on the temptation. I had to remain strong by being prepared for whatever temptation Satan was going to send my way. I remembered the bible told me that my body is a temple. He had forgiven me and restored my body so I was not willing to harm my body and soul again for anyone. No more roller coaster rides for me!

I remained cognizant of my escapes whenever temptations would arise in my life. The bible also tells us that when we are tempted, God will provide an escape for us. When you are in a moment of temptation and the phone rings, someone knocks on the door, you suddenly hear someone's voice in your head about this situation, or something makes a random startling noise, those are your escapes. Remember: **For every temptation, there is an escape.** *Pray* for an escape, *look* for the escape, and *take* the escape.

Renounce: *To renounce means to reject or abandon something; to break away from something; or to no longer accept participation in something.*

After you repent, it is crucial that you renounce all soul ties that have been chained to you as a result of engaging in sexual sins. When you renounce soul ties *through the power of God and the blood of Jesus*, you are released from the bondage that the soul ties once enchained you to. It is also important that you get rid of any possible materials, gifts, or any tangible tokens that were given to you during your involvement in the sexual sin with the other person. Many people don't realize that even though you have repented and have been forgiven, physical things can still hold the bond together between you and the other person that the sin was committed with.

Keep in mind that everything is spiritual; therefore, the objects symbolize a part of the unholy bond that brought you together. Although they prefer humans, demonic spirits can also attach themselves to objects. Recall the above references to Matthew 12 where we learned that demons do not like to wander around homelessly. They like to have a home. When they cannot get the person, they will attach themselves to non-human or inanimate objects (see Mark 5). If possible, destroy all objects associated with the sexual soul ties. This way, Satan cannot so easily use you as his instrument.

Recommit: *"But he that is joined unto the Lord is one spirit" (1 Corinthians 6:17).*

Remember, the bible tells us that we become one body with whomever we join bodies with. But when you repent and renounce those sins and sexual soul ties, you are made new by God. As a result, you are ready to recommit your body and soul back to God. To do this means to vow to God to become one with Him in spirit, taking into account that your body is a temple that Christ lives within.

Learn to let God love on you.

Talk to Him as much as you would talk to a guy. Tell Him about your day, your desires, and your inadequacies. It may sound silly at first, but I encourage you to go on dates with God. Receive love from God first. I guarantee after you allow God to love on you, you will look at relationships so differently. You won't continue to waste your time on men that constantly take from you. God is not a man that can lie. He won't make broken promises or reject you.

I promise God knows how to love you better than any man.

If you allow God, you will feel his love so real. God will fill every void and restore every empty hole that men have dug in you. How will you know unless you try Him?

This is the jumpstart in taking back your life.

If your life is out of control, the only way to get it back on track is to allow God to be in control. But you have to free His temple (your body) of other spirits that are not like Him so that His Holy Spirit can mightily dwell and work within you.

Once you recommit your life to Christ, He will make things that were meant for your bad turn out for your good (Romans 8:28). He will exchange your detours for His direction. He will turn your mistakes into miracles and your failures into successes. Trust me! I'm a witness that when you recommit your soul, heart, and body to God, He will catapult your dark trials into divine triumphs.

Once I recommitted my life to God, everything started falling right into place! The prosperity in my life has been a never-ending provision! The devil meant for my teenage pregnancy, the STDs, the issues at home and at school, etc. to take me out, but God turned it *all* around for my good!

My son has been one of the biggest blessings since the day he was born! My life didn't really begin until after he was born. It didn't really begin until after I joined God as one in spirit. God used my son in a mighty way to turn what the enemy meant for my bad into my good! I have been happily married to Rell (the one that fathered my son) for over twelve years now. As a result of our recommitment to God, our anointed marriage has been a flourishing fountain, ministering to thousands of people, young and old.

You will hear later about my education and prosperity that God continues to blow my mind with. All of this began with my son. God used him to mark the beginning of this prosperous new life that God had planned for me all along. God showed me that the fact that I stepped out of His will did not change His mighty plans and providence over my life. Once I stepped back into the will of God, my prosperous life began—with my son in my arms. Not only this, but my son has an unbelievable relationship with God for a young boy his age. He's a handsome, charismatic, straight 'A' student enrolled in all Pre-AP classes. He's also the most well-mannered, mature, and wisest young man I've ever seen!

My son is even one of the persons (the others being God and my husband) that helped inspire me to write this book. I told him how I had a tough story to tell and how God had healed me from all the pain in my past. He replied, "Stories were meant to be told mama. Your story will help so many people. God wants you to tell your story." Since a baby, he has always had this extraordinary wisdom about him.

The bond that we share is so spiritually strong that it heals and strengthens my soul. God did this! Since birth, I've known that my son's destiny was bigger than I could ever write about and I'm waiting to see it manifest! I was pregnant with destiny when I was seventeen; spiritually and literally. Without a doubt, in April of 2004, I gave birth to something *big*; my son and my destiny! Through my son is how I learned to allow God to love on me again.

God wants you to know that no matter how far you've fallen

from His will, if you recommit your life back to Him, He can take those shattered pieces of glass that represent your life and make it whole again! God says that His ears are not too heavy that He cannot hear our cries, but our sins can separate us from Him to the point where He hides His face and will not listen (Isaiah 59:1-2).

Your God-given destiny is still there. Your promised future is still available. God is just waiting on you to connect with Him and become one with Him again. Remember the three R's: *Repent* of your sins, *Renounce* your sexual soul ties, and *Recommit* your life (body and soul) back to Christ!

If you are ready to recommit your body back to God, turn the page. I've provided a recommitment pledge and embedded the three R's in it. You must mean it and believe it. If you say the prayer of the "Recommitment Pledge" from your heart and believe it, you will be immediately recommitted back to God and He will remember your sexual sins no more! You must continue to seek God and change your habits that led you to having sex. *Know that our own efforts are not enough.*

I have prayed for you! I'm excited for your new life; newfound power, and newfound freedom that you are about to experience! I'm rooting for you!

Most importantly, God is rooting for you!

Dear Diva,

Whenever you are ready to sign the Recommitment Pledge on the next page, it would do my heart well if you would send a copy of the pledge to the business address or email address below. This is strictly voluntary and may be used for data reports and ministry purposes.

Feel free to scratch out all names of sex partners.

Leave the bottom signature portion visible. If used, your first name will be concealed.

Thank you in advance for helping this ministry!
~Dr. Nioka

Dr. Nioka Smith Ministries
6104 Forbing Rd
Little Rock, AR 72209
Email: info@drniokasmith.com

Recommitment Pledge

by Dr. Nioka Smith|www.drniokasmith.com

Please make copies and use a separate pledge for each sex partner.
Repeat the prayer & pledge for each sex partner.
Do not remove or alter the title and copyright line above.

"No temptation has overtaken you except what is common to mankind. And God is faithful; He will not let you be tempted beyond what you can bear. But when you are tempted, he will also provide a way out so that you can endure it."
-1 Corinthians 10:13

Dear Heavenly Father,
I have committed fornication which is unholy in your eyesight. Please forgive me. I repent. I desire to be restored. I renounce all soul ties that were formed between ___state the name of the person you had premarital sex with___ and me as a result of premarital sex. By the power of the Holy Spirit, I break the chain of the sexual soul ties between ___state the name of the person you had premarital sex with___ and me. I break the agreement that my soul made with his soul when I had sex with him. The blood of Jesus sets me free (Ephesians 1:7); so with authority, I cut the cord that connects my soul to his soul. I take back possession of my soul and I expel the pieces of his soul that I've carried. May my body *reject* his soul in Jesus' name! I unite myself to you Lord to become one spirit with you and my husband only. Right now, I recommit my heart and body back to you. Today, I vow to refrain from sex outside of marriage. Please give me the grace to keep my vow. I pray that you will give me the wisdom to notice the escapes that you provide for me when temptations arise and grant me the willpower to take advantage of the escapes. It is done. In Jesus' name, Amen.

My body and soul are recommitted to God this _____ day of _____ 20_____.

Name _____

Signature _____

Please tear off and frame. Men won't reward you for this, but God will!

5

Wife Me Down

&

Ooh, he is ballin'!" "Did you see his car girl?" "He got that paper honey!" "That man stay on swag!" I hear these statements all too often. Focusing on those types of materialistic things will eventually lower your dignity or self-worth. Why? The things you chose above are your "driving forces". We tend to sacrifice a lot in order to gain the top things that we are driven by. I surveyed fifty women and girls between the ages of 14-35 inquiring of their desires for their ideal boyfriend/husband. Only five women mentioned something about a guy's values. When a guy's values are the "driving force" for women, there is not a lot that she has to sacrifice because he has his values in order. Some women are driven by the guy's looks. Some are driven by the cars he own or house he lives in. Some are driven by the amount of money he has and how he dresses. She sacrifices her dignity in order to receive what she is "driven" by. The woman begins to focus solely on the materialistic things such as his money, car, looks, style, the way he approaches her, his "swag", etc. These fruitless things (her vain driving forces) cause her to lower her standards. Don't get so caught up on materialistic and temporary things. Values are things that a person holds dear to them; their worth, and what they use to base their decisions on.

Values that should be considered are things such as:
    What are his beliefs?
    Does he value and honor God?
    What are his goals in life?
    Does he value education?
    Does he have a plan to graduate high school/college/trade school?
    Does he have a legitimate and realistic business plan?
    Is he ambitious and tenacious, not easy to give up?
    Is he patient and understanding, leaving no room for a hot-headed temper?
    What does he think about women in general?

Always remember that what's most important is not what the guy can do for you or solely how he makes you feel, but the significance is in his values. The truth of the matter is that if his values are up to par, then he will make you feel like a queen and will do a lot of great things for you because those things come as a part of his package. If he values women and girls and feels like they are precious jewels sent by God, then he will automatically buy you things that you want if he can afford them. He will automatically treat you like a queen. If he values education and has a plan to be successful in things other than drugs, guns, or gambling, then he will encourage you and refrain from bringing you down because his values are in line and he wants you to stay on track along with him. Whether you are ready for a husband or not, it is important to make sure that you think about the guys that you date in a long-term manner. Even if you don't think they will be in your future, it is very possible to end up "stuck" with a guy due to the decisions that you make. If the guy cannot offer what you need now, don't assume that he will be able to offer what you need in the future! That's a big mistake! Thinking about the values you want in a guy will cause less headache and heartache for you in the future. I titled this chapter "Wife Me Down" because if the guy doesn't fit into your future as your ideal husband, you should not waste your time on him.

"Wife Me Down" is when a man is capable of acknowledging your worth, and is ready to commit to a lifetime of cherishing your worth!

Can he possibly be the guy one day that marries you and gives you the life you desire and deserve? This is what I mean by "Wife Me Down". The phrase "Wife Me Down" is not just saying yes to a ring.

"Wife Me Down", according to the Divas Unchained principle, is when a man is capable of acknowledging your worth, and is ready to commit to a lifetime of cherishing your worth! Whether you are a teenager or adult, it's time to stop thinking short-term and think about your future and whether the guy is able to *wife you down* in the future.

It is imperative that you make every decision with a guy as if that guy was going to be in your life forever. You must make the decision regarding a guy as if he would be your future husband because you never know how things may turn out (*Below I will share a story that will explain this to you*). Most women today who jump from relationship to relationship do so because they do not hold any high standards for a guy.

Maya Angelou said it best, "When people show you who they are, believe them the first time." [1] What powerful words those are! So I beg you, look at who the guy is and believe that's all you will get from him. Don't try to make him be who you can *clearly* see he's not and then get angry at him and speak badly of him for being the man he has always been since the beginning of the relationship.

Approximately 55% of Black women Never marry. [2]

Five Marriage Misconceptions

The Most Common Misconception: *Marriage is only a piece of paper.*

Women say, "We don't need a piece of paper to define our commitment to each other." The devil smiles when he hears women say things like that because it's right where he wants us. Marriage is not only about being committed to each other; it's also about being committed to God. Marriage was orchestrated by God. Marriage contains God's signature on the sexual intimacy and the need for companionship that we were born with. Marriage is a reflection of God's covenant relationship with us. It demonstrates our love for one another in the pure way that God loves his people (the church). Marriage is not just a piece of paper; it is not just about the rings or wedding ceremony. It's about the joining of flesh between a man and a woman (Genesis 2:24); it is about them becoming one under God. Yes, it involves physical intimacy; but moreover, it involves spiritual intimacy. Marriage is designed to celebrate oneness. The piece of paper is not what denotes oneness. Taking marital vows in front of God does.

Lastly, marriage becomes a three-person bond where the almighty God is a member of the relationship (Ecclesiastes 4:12). How awesome! You can't get this covenant with fornication. To assume that marriage is only a piece of paper or to state that one feels like she is already married because of love is a complete insult to God and self. Marriage was instituted by God and designed as the most solid foundation for a family.

Misconception Number 2: *No man is going to control me!*

This is why you allow God to guide you in the right direction. You pray to God for the man whose rib you are; the man that God has designed just for you. You pray and wait on the man that understands that God is His head and that you are his soul mate, helpmate, and companion; taken out of his side, to be cherished. You pray for your husband before you even meet him that he will come to know and love God, so that he knows how to love you fairly and equally. Be patient and prayerful.

Misconception Number 3: *The woman always gets stuck!*

Women get stuck with too many kids, too many bills, and too many problems. The main benefit of marriage is that you have a third partner helping you through it all; a third partner with all power that is able to keep you, strengthen you, and prosper you. That third partner is God. "A person standing alone can be attacked and defeated, but two can stand back-to-back and conquer. Three are even better, for a triple-braided cord is not easily broken" (Ecclesiastes 4:12 NLT).

When you are married to your soul mate that God has chosen for you, you have a special anointing that covers you both, specifically because of your obedience and honor to God. Go into the marriage with God as your third cord and you will both be able to withstand all the darts of the enemy so that being stuck is not ever a concern.

Misconception Number 4: *You lose your freedom.*

What kind of freedom are these people looking for? Freedom to sin? Freedom to have sex with other men? Freedom to go where they want to go? A husband is a friend. In fact, he should be the best friend you will ever have in your life. And if he is the "Wife Me Down" type of man, you'll want to spend more time with your husband as a friend than your girlfriends anyway. Moreover, he will encourage you to enjoy yourself in ways that interest you, as long as they're harmless, and even when it doesn't include him. As mentioned in a previous chapter: when you're in sin, it's not really freedom anyway. Satan dresses it up so nicely that bondage looks like freedom. We really lose more when we suffer the consequences of our sins. The bible tells us "…If they can't control themselves, they should go ahead and marry. It's better to marry than to burn with lust" (1 Corinthians 7:9 NLT). As a result, marrying allows you to gain more than you lose.

Misconception Number 5: *Marriage causes you to lose your identity.*

Since marriage is designed to connect you with your soul mate, you actually gain the other half of your soul. If the man is truly your soul mate and husband sent by God, you will complete each other. He can help you see things about yourself in ways that you have never seen before. He can pull things out of you that you did not even know you had in you.

~

Before you were born, God had already designed your Adam, also known as your husband. In the spirit, He has already taken your future husband's rib out of him and made you from it. This is another reason women are to save themselves for their husbands. Please do not fall into the pattern of thinking that marriage is not important. I've heard one of my former friends say, "Girl, don't nobody get married anymore!" That's a stronghold of the devil.

You don't need to jump from guy to guy looking for a soul mate. In fact, you should not be the one looking for a man. Tell God your desires, pray, and watch. When the time is near, God will cause the man to find you as God has designed (Proverbs 18:22). Just make sure you're in the right location to be found, which is in God's will. Too often, women dress up in clothes that attract the "wrong" guys, go to the club, and say they're trying to find a man.

Please don't run after men and boys! When a woman does that, it is outside of God's will, tactless, and undignified. God wants women to focus on growing their relationship with him and building their character while he grooms their future husband. Here's a secret: sometimes, God wants you to allow Him to love on you himself so that when your husband comes, you'll already be prepared with knowledge on what pure and worthy love looks like!

Sex without Benefits

We now know that premarital sex is yet another stronghold that Satan bounds women with. Satan wants women to believe that there is no soul mate out there for them. He knows when women believe that lie, they settle for any man. He knows that when they hook up with men who betray and disrespect them, it usually affects any children involved, which can also affect the entire lineage (grandkids and great-grandkids). Sex without benefits can set a woman back pretty far in multiple ways. Satan wants women to believe that marriage is not important so that he can hold them hostage in their lives and keep them chained in their relationships. He knows that if he can get you to reject or resist the very thing that God ordained and honors, then he can keep you from reaching your goals as well as cause you to prolong your blessings from God. The Bible tells us that Jesus came to give us an abundant and satisfying life, whereas Satan comes to kill, steal, and destroy (John 10:10).

If he cannot wife you down, then he should move around!

A lady I knew lost her children's father to violence. They were still very much a couple at the time of his unfortunate death. They lived together with their kids. However, they were not married. The obituary mentioned his parents, kids, and close family members. However, at the end of the obituary, it read: "He also leaves behind a special friend, Justine."

Here she was the mother of his children, cooking for him, washing his clothes, taking care of them (playing family), and having a regular sex life with him, and she was not even listed as part of his family. Legally, she meant nothing to him. She could not make decisions about his life when he was in the hospital. She could not make decisions about his finances, or even have rights in the funeral arrangements. All of that was left up to his mother; someone who was recognized as his "family" by the law.

Even though she had kids with him, the legal system still recognized her as just a friend. This is humiliating! To top this off, she could not even receive any of his life insurance money because she was not married. Granted, a small portion of it went to the kids, but the bulk of it went to his mother who was the one to decide how much she wanted to disburse to the kids. Now she was left to raise the kids alone, with no financial security.

Single mother families are 5 times more likely to live in poverty than married couples. [3]

Married people that live for God receive bountiful blessings because they honor God. God honors marriage. In many scriptures, God promises to favor couples who are married among those who are not married (Proverbs 18:22). In Proverbs 31:10, we are informed that a woman who is married is known for her excellent worth. God refers to wives as fountains that flow with pleasure and joy and He promises that He will continuously bless the husband and his wife (Proverbs 5:18).

Wow!

Isn't it startling how much more we are missing out on when we weigh the two against each other: premarital sex and marital sex? Isn't it preposterous how Satan deceives us into believing that we are winning with the temporary pleasure that pre-marital sex offers—when in the end, we actually lose?

Satan knows it. He knows that temporary pleasure is what our flesh desires. This is why he makes it easily available to us so that we can miss out on the promises and benefits of marital sex.

You are not alone. You have read how I fell into Satan's trap. It looked like I was winning. I never realized all the chaos and consequences that could actually stem from it. Not only was I losing emotionally and physically, but I found that I was also losing legally and spiritually. The truth is: premarital sex comes with far more losses than benefits. The temporary pleasures of premarital sex don't compare to the benefits and victories of marital sex.

Don't give a man the benefits that only a husband deserves! What work has he done? What has he invested in you? If a man sees that he can get all the husband benefits without marrying you, he feels like, "What's the point?" I see too many women and girls (especially young women) giving men everything before he even makes a commitment. I see women raising other men's kids, cooking their meals, washing their clothes, sacrificing their happiness and futures, and giving them regular sex and all she gets in return is some random post on social media thanking her for putting up with his drama.

Just so you know, drama is translated as "unfaithfulness" and "disrespect" toward her.

The more recent benefit I've seen a woman give a boyfriend is the title "king". I am known for calling my husband my king in private and in public. That's exactly what he is to me just like I am his queen. But trust me, he has *earned* this title! He deserves this title and I am entitled to legal and spiritual benefits as his wife.

A boyfriend is not your king! Titles carry a lot of weight and significance. Calling him a king means you have given him the highest title a man can possibly have. The king is the head. So you've made him your head, and you are not even entitled to anything he owns (not legally or spiritually).

So now he has power with no commitment.

Where does that leave you?

Powerless and vainly committed.

This has to stop! If he cannot wife you down, then he should move around! And another thing: a 10-year long engagement is not an engagement. In fact, if it's been a *couple* of years and he still can't figure out you're the one worth marrying and committing to, then he should move around! My good friend often speaks about women accepting engagement rings when they are really *shut up rings*. My friend speaks the truth. Now, hear me clearly. I do **not** encourage or condone *shut up rings*. These are the rings that women receive from men so that she can stop pestering him about marriage.

Many times, he never has any intention on marrying her. However, sometimes the man will propose to her with a *shut up ring* so that she can keep quiet while he sleeps around with other women or continues to do whatever he wants to do. She shuts up because she has a ring and she is considered "Number One". Ms. Diva, being number one is not enough! Being Number one and the only one is what you are worth! Know your worth! Proclaim your worth! Save your benefits (including sex) for your husband and don't settle for a *shut up ring*! The moment you settle, you have lowered your dignity.

Marriage was created by God and is very honorable in his eyesight. Yes, marriages have struggles. However, if it is the *right* husband who was sent by God and if you are operating in His spiritual will, God will do nothing less than bless you abundantly.

Even if you have had a lot of sex partners, make a commitment to stop now and save yourself for your God-designed husband. Your God-designed husband will respect the fact that at least you made the decision to use self-control and become celibate. It's not too late for you! Repent and choose the new lifestyle of celibacy. It won't be easy. That's why you have to ask for God's power that lives within you to help you carry out the task (Ephesians 3:16-21 GWT). If you are a virgin, make a commitment now to stay a virgin until God sends your God-designed husband. Whether you're a virgin or not, he's out there. Work on yourself and your relationship with God first. Don't waste your time on alot of destructive or *temporary* relationships. Save this time to get your relationship solid with God so that He can release your "God-sent" husband to find you. God may just be waiting on you to work on yourself and show that you are *ready* for your husband.

Value Check

In order to secure your future and make it the most pleasant future possible, here are some questions you should ask yourself when dating: "Can this guy *effectively wife me down* in the future? Would he be able to meet my needs in the future?"

This means you will have to think about the values you want

your future husband to have. This way, when you date a guy, you will be able to scan your mental checklist (value checklist) to see if his values match your list.

Remember, materialistic things can vanish from the guy in the blink of an eye, but no one can take his values away. If he does not have the right values, he will either be uninterested or incapable of "wife-ing" you in the manner that you deserve.

Never make permanent decisions with temporary guys. All too often, women and girls think on a temporary level. The way they see it is that they are young and are just having fun and enjoying life. Satan desires to sift you like wheat and his desire is to demean you as just another female statistic who has been run down by multiple men; another female statistic that writes you off as bitter or scorn; or another female statistic that doesn't have what it takes to get married or stay married.

According to a recent article, "The U.S. marriage rate is the lowest it has been in more than a century." [4] The article further explains that since the 1950s, the rate of married women has decreased with the most dramatic decline being amongst *black* women at a 60% decrease. [4]

Your biggest hater, your most ruthless enemy doesn't want you to understand how much everything that you do with men and your body impacts your character and future. He doesn't want you to believe that God is holding a vast amount of blessings in His hands waiting on you to make the right decisions.

When dating a guy, do a "future glance" with your values checklist. Think about where you desire to be in life. Ask yourself about your goals and consider how this guy can fit into your future. Never assume that he will change. You cannot make anyone change. What are his goals? What plan does he have for his future? What are his values?

I know you may be saying, "Hey, I'm young. I don't have to

think about that now."

It's quite the contrary. Let me paint the picture for you.

Diva to Diva

✍

Brenda, a teenage girl started dating a guy named Timothy (Tim). This guy made her feel special. He gave her the attention that she needed because she had no father. He spent a lot of time with her and bought her some food every now and again. He even cooked frozen pizza for her sometimes. He was all hers. Living in a house full of kids and sharing a room with her siblings, Brenda finally had something that she could say was hers and she felt good about it. She thought of Tim all day long as she doodled their names on her school assignments while daydreaming in class. She knew that he smoked cigarettes, but that didn't stop the fact that he loved her and showed his love for her to everyone.

Brenda didn't know that Tim smoked crack.

He never let her see that part.

Brenda knew that he was in a gang, but she felt like that had nothing to do with her.

In her mind, she was still going to excel in school and continue making the A's and B's on her report card. She was going to go to college and become a registered nurse. She was very smart in math and absolutely loved science. Tim's gang involvement and smoking had nothing to do with her future life.

One day at the tender age of 15, she found out she was pregnant by Tim. Before she gave birth to their baby, he was convicted of theft and drug possession and sentenced to prison.

She raised the baby alone with the help of her mom and the assistance of welfare.

The baby's father was released from prison a few years later. The couple reunited. Brenda knew that she would have to stay in their small hometown and move into a project or Section eight welfare house with her baby and boyfriend. However, she made plans to stick it out, graduate high school, and go to a two year college. Her dream nursing degree would have to be put on hold for a while until the baby was much older. However, at the age of seventeen, a few months before high school graduation, she gave birth to a second baby. The father of the children, Tim, could not get a job because of his criminal record. They struggled to pay utilities and rent of $33.00 per month on a government home. The harder Timothy tried to get a job, the more he was rejected by employers.

Finally, he ended up robbing a store to get some money to support his family. He went back to prison. It is now ten years later, Brenda still hasn't received the college degree she had dreamed of. She has jumped from job to job trying to find decent pay. She has been in and out of college, adding and dropping classes hoping to one day graduate college. She is living in an apartment with her two fatherless children, working at two fast food restaurants just to try to make ends meet.

$$\mathcal{P}\infty$$

Do you get where I'm going? Several things were wrong.

Number one

Brenda focused too much on what the guy could do for her and how he *temporarily* made her feel rather than his values. He never valued education or achievement. He valued the drugs that he smoked and his membership in the gang. Yes, he loved her indeed, but his values were so toxic that they overpowered their relationship and his love for her. He did not have many positive values. Positive values help to improve relationships; toxic values deteriorate relationships. Because his values were toxic ones, they ended up putting him in situations that led him away from their relationship. Even with the true love that they had, his values caused permanent consequences!

=

Number two

Brenda's values were the complete opposite of his. She valued legitimate achievement; Tim didn't. She was an honor student with a plan to go to college. She valued a future career; he didn't. She would have never smoked anything because her "driving force" was education. For her, all other things in her life had to take the backseat.

The Bible says, "Do not be unequally yoked…" (2 Corinthians 6:14). He did not have the same values as she did; so therefore, they were unequally yoked. He did not attend church; moreover, he did not have a relationship with God. Brenda had a relationship with God. God doesn't want you to refrain from being nice to someone, but he does not want you to have an intimate relationship with someone that you are unequally yoked with. The scenario above with Brenda is evidence of why you should not be unequally yoked with someone.

Number three

Brenda made a permanent decision with a temporary guy. This guy was never going to successfully fit into her future. She never asked herself if he could be beneficial to her future. She knew where she was headed in life. This means she was given the signs that his future was very far from what she pictured her future as. The signs of smoking, stealing, and gangbanging were clear signs that his future included jail cells. By making this permanent decision, Brenda ended up pregnant; not once, but twice by a guy whose values never indicated that he would be an active father to a child. He did not value family in the way that she needed. He considered the gang members his family where they fought to show love.

Don't ever *sleep* with a guy who clearly shows signs that he does not fit into your future. As a matter of fact, Ms. Diva, never *date* a guy that indicates values different from yours. Don't waste your time! Once you fall in love; once you get chained to soul ties, it becomes very tough to move forward. Anytime you lower your dignity and have sex with a guy that has different values than yours, you are making a permanent decision. You cannot take the decision back and that decision brings about permanent consequences. Brenda's permanent consequences were teen pregnancy, an absent baby's father, and delayed goals. This guy was a temporary guy because he was never supposed to fit into her future. Never lower your standards or values to be with a guy. Put your dignity first. The guy may be temporary; but your decisions are permanent!

Reality Check

Again, whether or not you desire to get married, you should think long-term. Are you behaving in a manner that would make guys *want* to wife you? Perform a reality check because the way you carry yourself determines the response you get from guys. Your reputation follows you, even into your future relationships! Check your behavior to see if you are behaving in a way that would make a man *desire* to make you his wife.

Carry yourself in a way that makes a man say, "There is something too special about her to let her get away without me making her my wife!"

Diva to Diva

Cynthia was a very beautiful and extremely smart young lady. She always dressed nice, but never showed too much skin. How do you think the guys responded to her? They all respected her. Many of them secretly wanted to be her boyfriends. The same guys that wanted to be her boyfriends were the same guys who disrespected other women by having sex with them and then rejecting them, cheating on them, etc. However, they wanted to date Cynthia as one to take home to their parents and possibly "wife her down" one day. When she finally agreed to date a guy, he treated her like the queen she carried herself as.

What made Cynthia so different?

She had the whole package that would attract the type of guy that would treat her like a queen. The main quality that made this lady different was the fact that her beauty was not solely in the skin that she showed, but in the way that she carried herself. She was beautiful without showing her breasts, upper thighs, and underwear through her pants. However, she didn't dress like a nun or a tomboy. She dressed in a very fashion-forward manner and looked very attractive in her clothing.

Respectable, decent guys are drawn to these kinds of women. These girls give guys a challenge. They are not easily available. She didn't throw herself at guys. She did not expose herself as being available to almost any guy that approached her. She didn't portray herself as a man-thirsty, attention-hungry female. The guys were able to see her beautiful personality because they were not sidetracked by her butts, breasts, and thighs. She exhibited character that made her different and made her stand out amongst the others.

Now understand this, not as many guys approached her as they did the other young ladies who wore attention-hungry clothes and posted pictures showing off their backsides. You see, many men and boys alike already know that in order to approach this kind of woman or girl with great dignity for herself, they must have more to offer her and must be ready to put more energy and time into her. So, don't be saddened if not as many guys approach you as they do other young ladies. *Understand that your worth demands a particular type of attention and a special type of guy.* Be confident in knowing that not all guys are worthy of even approaching you. Count it a blessing!

There is a profound difference between a guy that just wants to sex you and a guy that wants to eventually marry you. Even if you are a long while away from being married, it is important that you carry yourself as a decent, respect-worthy lady. This is the way to get a guy to cherish you! Stay away from the attention-starving behavior whereby the clothes that you wear scream that you are hungry for sexual attention.

So many call themselves "wifey-type", but what exactly is wifey material?

God considers the following characteristics as a woman who is worthy:

She is humble, has a gentle and quiet spirit, and the *inside* of her body—which is her heart and soul—is so beautiful that it gleams onto the outside (see 1 Peter 3:4). She is no longer fascinated with the clubs and night life because her top priority is being able to make a home out of a house for her future husband and children—but she refrains from *playing wife* until she *actually is wife*. She understands balance and authority. She knows how to be meek, but maintain her strength all at the same time.

I call these last characteristics as the mother of all clues to wifey-material:

The young lady who is wifey-type never wastes her time on guys who she "knows" she would not want to spend the rest of her life with. Additionally, she will never waste her time on a guy that she knows cannot effectively "wife her down" in the future. She thinks about more than the "now". She thinks about her future and what the guy can bring to her future. She even considers how the guy would benefit her current or future children. She recognizes that it is a waste of her time to get with a guy that drinks excessively, smokes dope, sells drugs, curses his mom out, disrespects women, or has no ambitions for life. She simply performs a reality check or value check before getting herself waist deep into a chain of defeat.

The Movie of Your Life

When dating, take a moment to view your life as a DVD movie. With DVD movies, you can fast-forward them to see what happens later on in the movie or at the end of the movie. Occasionally, if the DVD is dirty or scratched, the movie will begin to skip scenes or completely stop. Some people attempt to take the disc out of the DVD player, clean it off and put it back in.

Most of the time, the DVD continues to skip scenes because there is too much damage done to the disc. They must then change the entire DVD in order to watch the movie efficiently.

The same applies to your dating life.

Sometimes, you need to fast-forward the DVD of your life with a guy to see what your future with him holds.

It may just be that he is too damaged with the wrong values. If this is the case, scenes in your life will be skipped.

That scene of where you graduate college may be skipped if the guy that you are dating has damaged or flawed values. The scene where you get your fairy-tale wedding and marriage may get skipped. That scene of your life where you enter into your dream career may get skipped because the DVD with this guy is scratched and damaged.

If you take the time to look at his values and fast-forward the DVD of your life with him, you will be able to determine if he will eventually keep your life at a standstill.

Being in a relationship with a guy that has damaged values can cause scenes in your life to be skipped in the same manner that a damaged DVD can cause scenes from the movie to be skipped. Depending on his values, he can keep your life from progressing. If you look at his values and realize that he is too damaged to begin with, do not even play that DVD. Pray to God to send the right guy with appropriate values according to His will.

My husband comes from a rough background, but he was always a guy with great values. Even as a teen, I was attracted to his values because even though he was poor (as was I), his values were rich! And today, those values of his have led to him earning a multiple six-figure yearly income. My Diva sister, don't look at the guy's money and swag without *first* looking at his values. **A man with great values is never poor!**

If you look at a guy's behaviors now and he is emotionally abusing you, physically abusing you, disrespecting his mom and other women, or smoking and drinking his life away, this is a clue of what your future would look like with him. Emotional abuse is when a guy says things to lower your dignity so that you will feel horrible about yourself and depend solely on him. If he puts you down instead of encourages you, keeps control of your belongings, refuses to let you spend time with your loved ones, or makes you think everything is your fault (even his mistakes), he is emotionally abusing you. It is a fact that emotional abuse can oftentimes have a much longer and deeper effect on a person than physical abuse.

If a guy disrespects his mom, trust me, it won't be long before he disrespects you.

Get this: if he's a momma's boy, would never disrespect his mom, but disrespects all other women, take that as a warning sign as well. Many times, women and girls seek the temporary things and totally refuse to think about the permanent things. They see the guy that can possibly give them what they are looking for at the present moment and that's all they think about. Don't get so hung up on what a guy can do for you at the present moment. *Think about what he can do for you in the future moments.* The same guy that seems to have it all right now while he is living with his mom may have nothing at all five years from now. Trust me, I've seen it all. I've seen guys that come from wealthy families, were really popular and nice-looking in the past, but when I look at them now, many people would call them bombs.

I say unto you again:

Do not focus on materialistic things such as money.

Things are not always cracked up to what they seem to be. This happens all too often with our women and girls today. They lower their standards and change their character for a guy that is not even worth it.

You should always pay attention to the values of a guy.

What is so dear to his heart? Is it God? Is it his mother?

His future career? His goals?

If so, then great, because all of these things are permanent things of great value. Stay away from guys who value temporary things such as being consistently focused on popularity, making "fast" money, spending all of his money on flashy cars and rims, fighting,

smoking, or hanging with his unambitious homeboys.

Take this time to evaluate at least three *values* that a guy must have before you begin dating him. Remember, leave materialistic things out of it. You can have a separate list for those if you'd like as your secondary list. Think of the DVD of your life. If it's in God's will, your God-sent husband is out there. Be prayerful. Be patient. Be watchful. You are a Diva with Dignity! The way I see it: if he is not the one to wife you down, then he should move around.

You decide!

Wife me down?

Or move around?

VIRTUE

TWO

The 'I' In DIVAS

INSPIRATION

"The quality or state of being [empowered to conquer, to be inspired, and to inspire others.] A force or divine influence that inspires someone."

Key Bible Scripture

"For our present troubles are small and won't last very long. Yet, they produce for us a glory that vastly outweighs them and will last forever!"

~II Corinthians 4:17 NLT

6

Life's Lemons

❧

One of my favorite quotes is, "When life gives you lemons, make lemonade." The lemons refer to adversities, trials, disappointments, and mistakes that occur in your life. The lemonade refers to your blessings, miracles, prosperities, or triumphs. *Therefore, turning lemons into lemonade means going from the victim to the victor!* The dictionary defines victim as "one that is subjected to oppression, hardship, or mistreatment." A victor is "a winner; one that defeats an enemy or opponent." Oppression is another word for persecution. You are a victim when you are persecuted in any way. You are a victim when you experience things such as rape, abuse, neglect, betrayal, poverty, teen pregnancy, sexually transmitted diseases, etc. Whether it is an alcoholic mother, absent father, abusive loved one, drug addicted sister, abandonment, betrayal by a loved one, a poor neighborhood, a run-down house, a lack of food, or scarcity in clothes, you are or have been a victim. All of these are examples of a victim because they all make a person subjected to oppression, hardship, or mistreatment. However, when you respond with faith, prayer, and praise as I will discuss in a later chapter, you begin to realize that you don't have to be a victim too long. You are about to find out how I went from victim to victor.

Please brace yourself for the story you are about to read. You'll see that it's pretty intense as you read on.

Diva to Diva

I was raised in a small town called West Helena, Arkansas. I have two brothers and two sisters that I was raised with. I am the fourth child out of five children. My oldest sister was pregnant with her first baby when she was fifteen and her second baby when she was sixteen. My mom raised us all on her own including the two grandchildren. We had very little money. There were times that my mom worked two jobs to get the bills paid. My daddy was in prison for about six years in Illinois. He left when I was about six or seven years old. After my father left and went to jail, things turned upside down in our house. My mom was the best mom in the world. She instilled the word of God in me. My mom took us to church every single Sunday there was. In the evenings, she held Bible study with us. Sometimes, we would have to catch the van to church at 7:00am when we didn't have a car. She was present at every award show and school event I had. However, it became difficult for her to raise my two older brothers with no father figure. A couple years after my dad went to prison, my brothers got involved in gangs. I remember our house getting shot up a couple of times; once, we ducked and fell to the ground just in the nick of time.

My brothers were in and out of jail and my mother was still doing everything she could, but to no avail.

Eventually, the gang involvement led to drugs. My brothers got addicted to cocaine drugs and things got even worse. I will never forget the day one of my brothers shot at my sister throughout her house because of the high from the drugs. I can remember the time my other brother hit my sister in her head with an iron pipe.

As she fell to the ground, the blood rushed from her head, and she began jerking.

All I could do was freeze.

At the hospital, the doctor said she should have had memory lost or amnesia, but God's amazing grace covered her.

We moved quite a bit following my father's incarceration. In fact, I remember when we lived in a small boxlike duplex house within an alley. This memory is so clear because of all the drug addicts, alcoholics, and criminals that dominated the streets of that alley every single day and night. There was a lady with AIDS who was on crack. My mom used to minister to her and give her food. One of those crack-heads broke into our house in broad daylight when I was there alone with my baby sister. As a little girl at the time, I was horrified when I saw his face come through our bathroom window.

Once, my brother tried to burn my other brother up as he set some curtains on fire and threw it on my brother while he was asleep. One of my brothers has literally tried to kill himself.

There was a time that he literally hung himself.

Another time, he drank an entire jug of bleach.

One would think he would die from hanging himself;

apparently, it wasn't his time to go. The list of suicidal attempts goes on.

If these things were not enough, the father of my sister's kids used to abuse her right in front of us. He would beat her so badly that I literally feared he was going to kill my sister. Before my daddy went away, he kidnapped me from school when I was about five or six years old. I never made it to my classroom that day. He told me we were going to Detroit, but it turns out I was only in Memphis, Tennessee. For a few days, I was so happy because I thought I was just on vacation with my daddy. I don't have a clue whose house we were living in and I remember things seemed a little awkward; something was not quite right. I remember hearing something about my daddy wanting some money in exchange for me. My mommy worked her maternal power some kind of way and found us and brought me home safely.

Fast forward into 1998, my dad was released from prison and came back to live with us. At this time, I was super crazy about my daddy. I always thought I was daddy's little girl. Before he went to prison, he always spoiled me because I was the baby at the time. So you can imagine how excited I was to have my daddy home again. When I was a little girl, I would sit in church every Sunday imagining him walking through the church doors surprising us. I played this wishful memory in my mind every single Sunday for six years. My daddy used to love surprising us, and I loved when he did it.

I was surprised alright. When he came back, we clashed immediately. He literally turned our house upside down.

It wasn't before long that he also got back on crack cocaine.

He was a drug addict and an alcoholic all over again.

He verbally and physically abused my mom right in front of me. I can see so vividly the memory of my daddy picking up the heavy, wooden living room table to throw at my mom as she ran out of the house and down the street in the middle of the house. It was around 2:00 am. Until this day, I can still hear the terror of my mom's voice from her screams that night.

So many days, I went to school very emotionally and physically exhausted. No one knew what I was dealing with. There were times my dad prevented my mom from going anywhere as he would do things like take a bat and beat the motor under the hood of her car to where we were without transportation.

Once, my mom completely vanished for weeks.

No one knew where she was. My little sister and I were still staying at the house with our father. He told us that he didn't know where she was. I was terrified out of my mind that my mom was going to be found in the woods somewhere dead. Finally, my grandmother caught word that her daughter (my mom) was missing. She came over to our house with a gun and told my father if she found out that he hurt her daughter in any way, she was going to shoot him. He swore he had no clue where my mom was. My granny then took us with her until my mom reappeared.

50% of American families are affected by domestic violence. [1]

Then, there's that all too familiar memory when my mother, father, little sister and I were in the car and my father threw my mom out of the car and threatened to take us away from her just out of pure hatred. My daddy took my mother's set of car keys and house keys from her and threw them into the woods and sped off leaving my mother in the road.

I could see the fear in my mother's eyes.

It was not fear of being injured, but the fear of losing us.

All of a sudden, my mother ran and jumped onto the speeding car. The car (with my father behind the wheel) dragged her down the road as she hung on to the door of the car in an attempt to not let us out of her sight. Half of her body was inside the car and half of her body was outside the car, on the ground, as the car sped down the road.

My little sister and I were the only two kids that were not adults. At this time, my oldest siblings were no longer living at our house and didn't see all the abuse and torture that my daddy caused us in our house.

I felt so helpless and hopeless.

I could not help my mother.

I cried to God,

"How could he do this to such a God-fearing, loving woman as my mother?"

I didn't understand; my mom is literally super kind to everybody: strangers and family alike. Everyone that knows my mother will tell you how meek, selfless, faithful, loving, and spiritual she is. Even in the midst of all of this, she remained strong in her faith to God.

Although the majority of my daddy's abuse toward me was verbal, he physically abused me a few times as well. Once, he knocked me on the kitchen floor when I was washing dishes. He called me all kinds of "b" names, whores, and mother [bleeps].

He always said to me,

"You will be pregnant before you are 15."

When I turned 15, he would say,

"You will be pregnant before you are 16."

He said it every year as if I was promiscuous or something.

I wasn't.

He never really worked, but he controlled the house in a way that instilled fear and discomfort in all of us.

My dad constantly threatened us...

"If y'all ever go to the police on me, this family will be on the front page of the newspaper. This is not a threat. It's a promise."

I was literally scared for my life as well as the lives of my mother and siblings. Would I wake up one morning and find my mother dead? I was so afraid to go to sleep. There were countless days that I went to school so sleep-deprived.

My mother could never put him out of the house on a long-term basis. The police said it was because they were married. The few times that my mom succeeded in kicking my dad out of the house, he would come back and break into the house— break a window or two, or break both doors to the house. There was a time that our front door and back door were both broken. My mom could not afford to fix them for a while, so we had to sleep in a house where the doors would not lock and could barely even close without putting a chair under the doorknobs. My little sister and I were scared out of our minds to go to sleep. We would not only fear burglars, but fear that my daddy would come kill us.

My mother tried getting a divorce several times.

Two things were wrong with this: he would not agree to a divorce and she could not afford a divorce. She had to go through some kind of free legal assistance which took over two years to approve a divorce. There was not one time that I felt safe when my daddy was home.

It's a sad fact, but I felt much safer when he was locked up and absent from us.

I can recall my daddy smoking a crack pipe right in front of me. As a matter of fact, he drove me into some dark woods, and sat there and smoked it in front of me. When he was drunk, he would keep my mom and I up all night on school nights as he found something to argue about in order to threaten us.

My daddy woke me up if I was asleep and threatened my life for no reason at all. He would point his finger in my face and put his face very close to my face with the most evil look. He would try to provoke me to say or do something out of order so that he would have an excuse to become more violent toward me.

I was afraid when I went to sleep and afraid when I woke up.

The man that was supposed to keep me from harm inflicted harm upon me.

Not only that, but the man that was supposed to provide for me actually took from me.

We had a huge deep freezer where my mom bought a lot of food from food stamps and stacked the freezer with meat.

So many times, my daddy sold the meat in the freezer for some crack cocaine.

In fact, he sold many of the items in our house for crack cocaine. My mom would have to scrap and figure out a way to feed us.

I was in a pre-college program called Upward Bound where they paid us stipends for making good grades. I always tried to help my mother around the house because she worked **so** hard and never received any help from my daddy or anyone else. I bought her a vacuum cleaner so that she would not have to sweep all that carpet with a broom anymore. My dad sold the vacuum for crack cocaine.

He sold my bed for crack cocaine.

My mom had just bought my little sister and me some new bikes. We were super happy with them as we had wanted them for a long time.

We didn't have them long because my daddy sold our bikes for crack cocaine.

We were so hurt. My daddy never bought me much because

he never worked. However; once, he bought me a radio for birthday. I had wanted that radio for so long.

He took it back and sold it for crack.

Once, he gave me $75 and asked for it back so he could buy some crack. He sold the lawnmower, bedroom set, and more so that he could smoke crack. Whatever we had in the house of value that he could get his hands on, he sold it for crack. I wish I could tell you that the story stopped here, but it gets worse.

My dad made me get undressed in front of him.

No matter how uncomfortable I felt, he forced me to take off my pants in front of him.

It was my punishment for sleeping in my regular clothes.

Although he forbade it, I slept in my regular clothes anyway because I felt very unsafe and uncomfortable around him. I didn't feel comfortable if I wasn't fully dressed when I slept at night. There was something shifty about the way he looked at me when I walked by. I always saw him looking at me in a way that was not pure; a way that was not innocent.

In an effort to ease my mind and get some sleep at night, I slept in my clothes. He said it was my punishment to get undressed in front of him. He sat directly and very closely in front of me as he carefully watched me undress myself under his authority. When I was finally undressed, he made me stand there with only my panties on.

While he argued at me for sleeping in my regular clothes, he attentively perused my lower body parts with his eyes.

There was one time when my daddy locked my mom in the bathroom and my dad forced me into my brother's old room onto the bed with a condom in his hand. He then closed the door and waived the condom in his hand while looking at me and walking toward me. My oldest brother came home to our house in the nick of time and my daddy ran out of the room.

I didn't tell anyone because I knew my brother would literally hurt my daddy or worse. I did not want my brother to go back to jail. I wish the next time I was lucky; but I wasn't.

The next time that my daddy attempted to sexually abuse me, he succeeded.

~

I WAS FOURTEEN YEARS OLD. It was one summer while school was out and my mom was at work. School was still in for my little sister, so it was just my dad and me at home. My daddy called me into their bedroom.

He told me to lie down beside him. I resisted. He forced me under his duress.

He then forced me to take off my pants and panties while lying beside him.

He grabbed my hand and forced me to rub my hand up and down his penis.

He then got on top of me and kissed and sucked on my breasts.

No matter how much I resisted and cried for him to stop, he took my hands and held them to where I could not move.

He yelled, "I'm your daddy and I said stop fighting!"

He then moved his finger up and down inside my vagina and penetrated my vagina with his fingers. Then, he sucked his fingers. He repeated these actions over and over from the sucking of my breasts to the finger penetration of my vagina to sucking my vaginal secretions off his fingers.

As I laid in that bed with his two hundred-plus pound body

on top of my under-developed small ninety-pound body, I thought to myself:

"This is the bed that he and my mother sleep in, lay naked in, and have sex in."

Nevertheless, there I was in the bed forced by my own biological father to do things with him that he did with my mom. My own father forced me to rub his penis in an ejaculation motion. He made sure I did it precisely and repeatedly, guiding me under his coercion in the motion he wanted me to go.

My own father kissed my breasts, fingered me, performed foreplay on me, moaned and groaned at the taste of my vagina and the fondling of my body, and forced me to masturbate him.

My own birth father sexually abused me.

After it was over, I picked up the phone to call the agency that my mother worked for. In the middle of me talking to the receptionist, my daddy caught me and asked who I had just called. I lied like I had called my friend Taz. He picked up the phone and hit redial. He heard it was my mother's job, so he hung up the phone.

He threatened me with his eyes.

He then went down the street to the store. I ran to my uncle's house.

I ran so fast that I didn't even look left or right for traffic.

I didn't look back.

I didn't stop to catch my breath.

Not thinking that my daddy would know where I had run off, I went to the market store across from my uncle's house with my cousins.

The next thing I knew, my daddy came after me with a bat and dragged me down the street, across the highway, and back home.

Something died in me on that day at the age of fourteen, and I never tried to discover what it was.

I buried the part of Nioka that had died along with my secret because my dad had threatened me not to say a word.

I was sorely afraid. I didn't want my brothers to be killed and I definitely couldn't live without my mother.

What's ironic is that I kept my mouth sealed so that my daddy wouldn't kill my family, but as you will see:

Over a course of fourteen years, the secret, pain, emptiness, and shame were actually killing *me*.

ℬ

In families where the father assaults the mother, the daughters are at risk of sexual abuse 6.5 times greater than girls in non-abusive families. [2]

My Life's Lemons

When I see other women with their fathers and proudly speaking of their dad as their hero; how they went out to dinner together; how he is always there for them emotionally and physically, it makes me feel cheated.

I don't know what it's like to feel comfortable in a room alone with your father.

I don't know how it feels for your daddy to innocently kiss you on the cheek or forehead without him becoming sexually aroused by your body.

I can't tell you how it feels for your biological daddy to hug you without wondering if he wants to take your clothes off.

I don't know what it's like to have a father give without expecting anything back.

How does it feel to have a father that doesn't use you to get what he wants?

I would imagine it's an incredible feeling to hear your father call you important rather than tell you you're nothing.

Oh what I would've given to hear my father call me his angel or princess rather than a bitch or whore.

What does it feel like to have a father constantly instill in your head that you will be prosperous instead of pregnant?

I still remember when my father found out that I was pregnant at the age of seventeen with my son. I had flashbacks of all those times that my daddy projected that I would be pregnant at fourteen, fifteen, and then sixteen. Everyone else knew of my pregnancy except him because he had disappeared again for a few months and returned. For months, I hid my belly from my daddy under a big pink bath robe because I was afraid of him finding out. Of course, he had sexually abused me about three years prior to my pregnancy and truthfully, I felt like he didn't have the right to be angry at the fact that I had gotten pregnant by a boy in high school. However, I was scared out of my mind of what he would do to me or what kinds of hurtful things he would say to me. My heart couldn't take another ounce of his rejection. Sure enough, when he found out by my grandfather that I was pregnant, he called me a whore and a bitch again. After calling me every foul curse word in the book, he then looked me directly in my eyes and said to me, "BITCH, YOU AIN'T SHIT!" Those words struck me like lightning. The pain caused by my father's words was excruciating. At that point, I had taken all I could take! I yelled at him and cursed back at him with so much hurt and anger that I stormed out of the house and fell flat on my pregnant belly. As my mother ran to me with tears, I looked up from the ground at my daddy's merciless face and decided at that moment that I could no longer live in a house with a father that engages in a sexual act with me, then get upset at me for being pregnant. On this night, I left my mother's house, seventeen and pregnant, to live with my seventeen year old cousin who had two kids of her own. I experienced a point of lowness and loneliness that no high school child should ever feel.

I could no longer live in a house with a father that engages in a sexual act with me, then get upset at me for being pregnant.

45% of pregnant teens report a history of sexual abuse. [3]

Even as an adult, I still dreamed of having an innocent father/daughter relationship with my father. I used to dream of him taking me to the father daughter dances, walking me down the wedding aisle and giving me away, being the one I can lean on when I'm in a bind, crying to him as he wipes my tears and reminds me how important and worthy I am. Up until my revelation from God (which I will share with you later), I dreamed of being able to go over his house as a getaway when I was stressed.

I always wanted to say, "Well, I'm going over my daddy's house so I can kick my shoes off, relax, go in the refrigerator, have my daddy to cook for me and spoil me, and be at my own 'home away from home."

I dreamed of feeling secure with my daddy and at peace around him instead of wondering if he's thinking *innocently* of me or *incestuously* of me.

For over two decades of my life, I held on to nothing but hope that turned into pain and emptiness.

Hope that ended up in my daddy's crack pipe or jail cell.

Hope that was swallowed up in the bottles of his gin and juice.

Hope that was consumed by my father's pride.

Hope that was stolen by the demons of my father's past.

As time went on, my father missed my high school graduation and both college graduations. He missed every last one of my children's births and every milestone moment in my life. One would think that I would not have had a relationship with my father being that he sexually, emotionally, verbally, and physically abused me. However, many people are quite appalled to find out that it was quite the opposite.

My daddy and I had a relationship well into my adulthood where contact was ongoing. He never missed a birthday. No matter which city he roamed to, he kept in contact with me. We laughed and joked all the time about how much alike we are. We had fun as we competed with each other by watching Jeopardy, discussed the Bible, etc. He bought my kids a bunch of snacks and goodies with his food stamp card as his way of doing something for the kids since he never really worked a job. When he received money, he always gave us a portion. He stayed in contact with all of his kids and we stayed in contact with him. He even moved to town to be closer to us many years ago.

As time went on and as years went by, I slowly realized that he was doing way more taking than giving. Many times, I picked him up and took him places because he never really had transportation. I was extremely proud when he got off drugs.

I thought, "Yes! Maybe now we can have the father-daughter relationship that I've always dreamed of."

Unfortunately, he was soon back on drugs.

I remember driving around looking for him because I missed him. There was this abandoned house that my daddy lived in. It was all boarded up with no lights, water, heat, or air. He and other drug addicts snuck in there at night to sleep. I went to the condemned house one day, but he wasn't there. I drove around and found him in the neighborhood doing drugs.

My adult nephew was in the car with me and gave him five dollars to get some food. I told my daddy I loved him, drove off, and wiped my nephew's tears. Although my nephew had known of my daddy's history of drug addiction, he had never seen it in action. This wasn't new for me. It was twenty years of seeing my daddy hanging on the street corners, living as a vagabond, lips discolored from the crack pipes, eyes glazed, speech slurred, excessive weight loss that made him smaller than myself, and being so distant from who he actually is on the inside.

I often invited him to church. He came a few times, but his demons are so strong that he runs from God a lot. He has run from his spiritual calling for decades now. I continued to do for my daddy as much as I could with a family of my own. I bought him food, drove him around to run errands often, gave him a few dollars from time to time, and even allowed him to stay at my house a couple of the times that he was homeless.

My daddy always played the guilt trip on me.

He manipulated me and used my godliness and kindheartedness against me. He also knew how crazy I was about him. A big part of me also feels like he knew I would do anything just to keep him in my life.

All I seemed to ever feel from him was rejection.

I always felt like I was never good enough or nothing I did was ever good enough.

My daddy made me feel like he loved me *if* I did something or *if* I said something a certain way.

Being in a father-daughter relationship with him caused me much grief, rejection, hurt, emptiness, and lowliness over and over. This was mainly because even after I had forgiven him, he still rejected me by hanging up on me when he was upset or by not listening to me when I tried to tell him about my stressors.

My father constantly said hurtful things such as he didn't want to have anything to do with me when he didn't get his way from me.

One would think that all these years, after he had caused all the pain from drug addictions, alcoholism, and his abuse toward us, that he would come around more, be more supportive, and do less manipulating. You would think so, since I had stayed in his life past all the pain that I still endured as a result of his actions.

So why did I continue to tolerate my daddy's shenanigans

even well into my adulthood, even after he constantly manipulated, rejected, used, and abused me?

I felt powerless when it came to my daddy because I was a victim of abuse and the abuser has control over the victim.

You see: People that have been abused have a very difficult time saying no to people, especially their abuser. It began when the abuser coerced himself on the victim. That was physical control. However, within that physical control comes emotional and psychological control. Since the abuser has control over the victim as a result of the abuse, the victim usually reverts back to the abuser.

You may know a woman or have heard of a woman in an abusive relationship with her boyfriend who keeps going back to the abusive relationship. We tend to call her ignorant, but we don't realize that the abuser inflicted control over that woman. Breaking free takes more than what one might assume.

Basically, my daddy instilled in me that no matter how much harm he caused me, no matter how it's tearing my soul apart, no matter how much my health is deteriorating as a result of his actions, I better put up with it. I better not say no or even think about resisting.

God revealed to me that I was holding on to the hands of the seven year old girl's father that used to protect her in *love* and *innocence* as they walked across streets. However, those hands (that protected me and loved me purely as a seven year old) had let my hands go and grabbed hands with crack, cocaine, alcohol, sexual demons, and more. But I stood at the door every day waiting on that same daddy to return. That daddy was gone; but in my mind, I was still hoping and wishing for that same relationship. Yes, even well into my twenties.

I was stuck!

It was indeed a spiritual stronghold that I had to break with the power of the blood of Jesus.

I was in chains!

In shackles!

It was an unholy and unhealthy spiritual soul tie between my daddy and me. Tragically, this was impacting me—spiritually, psychologically, and physically.

Throughout my youth and adulthood, I felt inferior to people of authority and very uncomfortable around men because of what my daddy did to me. As a result, when dealing with others in authority, I was anything **but** confident. I felt anything **but** worthy. All my life, I had attached myself (unknowingly) to my daddy as my source to give me back my self-worth, my confidence, and my voice. It wasn't until I attached my image, self-worth, and confidence to God that I regained it all back. God even gave me my voice back that was so violently stolen from me.

Spiritual Resume

Over the years, I have been attacked on every end regarding my destiny, family, marriage, and health. The attacks have been powerful and relentless. These attacks were in addition to what you have previously read regarding my upbringing: gang violence, drug addicted home, domestic violence, sexual abuse, etc. Shortly after my nephew's father was tragically gunned down, my nephew was shot next to his heart. The doctors said the bullet was a millimeter away from his heart and that he probably would not survive surgery. Glory be to God that he is still alive today. Shortly after that, my brother was wrongly convicted of a crime that he did not commit and sentenced to life in prison without parole. As if this were not enough, my baby sister suffered a major arterial stroke at the tender age of nineteen. She was at my house when it happened and my husband found her on the floor of our kids' bathroom. Although a miracle that she survived, she suffered major loss of her speech capabilities, loss of the function in her right arm, limited ability in her right leg, and damage to her brain. As close as my sister and I are, this was one of the most trying times of my life.

Needless to say, all of these things took a major toll on me.

Many people say to me, "Girl, you are so smart! How in the world did you achieve two college degrees with three kids?"

I tell them that I had to become focused on something or else I would have gone insane. They think I'm talking figuratively when I say that, but I'm not.

I have literally almost lost my mind before, more than once. At one point, I was seeing things, hearing things, thinking people were about to break into my house, thinking every man I saw was going to snatch me and rape me. I would hear voices (from Satan, of course) saying that I was going to die, that my mother and kids didn't love me, etc. Yes, I was losing my mind. Literally. These thoughts tortured me when I went to bed and when I awoke. It was because of all the turmoil I had gone through. But, God kept me!

I couldn't be in another room with a man without cringing and feeling like the little girl again who had to hide her breasts when in the same room with her daddy. I remember being in a room with the camera man that was only doing his job by videotaping my interview. As a result of the noise in the hallway, he had to close the door. I couldn't even focus because of the flashbacks from when I was sexually abused.

Little did I know that all of these episodes were symptomatic of a disorder that I did not know I had. I experienced these symptoms for *years* before finally being diagnosed with Post

Traumatic Stress Disorder (PTSD) which is when someone who was extremely traumatized keeps reliving the same traumatic events.

The episodes returned to where I could not sleep for fear that someone would break in my house just like my dad and strangers had done when I was a teenager. I feared someone would sexually abuse my daughters the way my dad had done to me. I would not sleep unless they were in the bed with me. I couldn't walk alone without fearing that someone would come behind me and rape me.

Every time I heard a noise, I jumped! I was so accustomed to emergency situations within my family (brothers' gang involvement or some other trouble, near death experiences of my brothers, father's domestic violence, sister's abuse by her boyfriend, etc.) that I always felt like something terrible was about to happen.

I could not sleep. When I heard certain noises, I would automatically think it was from gunshots as it occurred during my childhood when people would shoot in our house. I became so nervous inside that I was shaky all over. I began knocking over everything that I came in contact with. I could not fix dinner for my children or even pour a glass of water without spilling it.

Things got even worse before they got better.

Recently, my dad suffered a massive heart attack whereby he lost eighty percent of his heart function.

He almost died right in front of our eyes several times and slipped into a coma.

He experienced about eight surgeries in less than ten weeks.

When he was released, he was re-hospitalized almost every two days. I was the only person that could *legally* make medical decisions for him. Being his oldest biological daughter, I received phone calls from the nurses and doctors like clockwork to make decisions for him. Initially, I was at the hospital almost every day. I did not realize the impact that this would soon have on my health. Even though I thought I was getting better, my body soon revealed to me that I was not.

During my dad's severe illness and multiple near death situations, I found myself repetitively collapsing on the floor without a moment's notice.

I could not hold my body up.

I would get so weak and lose total control of my body to where I would just fall to the floor. This happened several times. My hands and feet continuously went completely numb without notice. Because of my unstable nerves and shaky hands, I dropped almost everything I touched, cut myself wrapping Christmas presents, burned myself several times, and accidentally stabbed myself with a knife while trying to open something.

The occurrences of the painful sexual abuse flashbacks intensified.

I had vivid, flashbacks of my daddy climbing on top of me and sexually abusing me.

I was tormented when I went to sleep and when I awoke. It was well over a decade later, and I could still feel my father's penis in my hands.

I see why people cut themselves.

I understand why others use self-mutilation as a coping method. Because as unbelievable as it sounds, during those piercing flashbacks, I severely wanted to cut my left hand off!

But God!

According to my therapist, my PTSD symptoms intensified as a result of my daddy's heart attack.

Whenever he was unconscious and I looked at him, I had illusions of him rising out of the hospital bed and attacking me as he used to do when I was a teenager.

Obviously, this could not be happening with him being in a coma, but the illusions were real inside of me.

There were times at the hospital when he was awake, smiling and playing, but I would all of a sudden see him frowning at me and calling me whores and the "b" word while trying to abuse me.

Even though I know he was actually smiling, I relived the painful past and saw him attacking me right in the hospital room. His face was literally transfigured before my very eyes; from a smile to that evil frown that he would give me when he was getting ready to threaten me as a child.

The more time that passed by, the worse the PTSD episodes became. I experienced the same fear over as if it was thirteen years prior. I was told that the PTSD and anxiety victims do not have the fight/flight response.

I agree because when I relived the painful events, I could not argue, yell, or defend myself (fight); neither could I run away from the room (flight). Therefore, I just felt a lot of anxiety trapped within my body. I experienced and saw things happening that were not actually happening. My therapist and primary care physician diagnosed me with PTSD, severe anxiety and clinical depression.

My insides rattled nonstop *every day*.

I had bowel movements about seven times per *day*. The devil relentlessly fed me evil and frightening thoughts about my dad dying, my family falling apart, losing my mind, etc. I could barely even take care of my children!

At this point, I had suffered depression before, but never had I suffered severe anxiety to where even my *teeth* rattled persistently and my insides jangled without ceasing. My hands shook ceaselessly and I could barely breathe due to hyperventilation. There was pain shooting through my nerves and I felt nervousness every single day—almost nonstop. The doctor prescribed me all kinds of medications such as tranquilizers and more.

I remember the doctor's words clearly: *"You need the tranquilizers to calm your nerves because you have gotten yourself in a position to where you can barely function as a human."*

~

I was having a real-life nervous breakdown. The doctors had to take me off work because I could not care for students in that condition. All of this happened at the same time! Can you imagine having three small children to care for while experiencing these trials? It literally took me over a year to recover after the nervous breakdown.

All I could say was,

"God, isn't it enough of what I've already been going through?
Why *this* God? I know whatever I'm going through,
there is a purpose and a plan for it. But God,
I can't even see a light at the end of the tunnel!
God, I am about to break into pieces!
Why must I suffer all of this at once? Why?"
God answered me in a reassuring voice,
"I'm building your spiritual resume."

Wow! How powerful!

I knew in my spirit exactly what God meant. A resume includes all your skills, education, experiences, and accomplishments. A resume is what is used to qualify you for a certain job or promotion. I have experienced illnesses, but never on this level. I had experienced blow after blow and trial after trial. God told me in order for me to qualify for the next level of ministry and elevated success, I had to have experienced what it feels like to have a nervous breakdown on top of the severe medical issues, father's health issues, and family issues. Even though I have always experienced non-stop spiritual attacks from the enemy my entire life, I had to learn the skills for dealing with Satan on an *even deeper* level.

God had to teach me how to deal with the unrelenting attacks from the enemy so that I could add this to the *experience* portion of my spiritual resume. He added another level of warfare to the *skills* section of my spiritual resume. He was telling me that when I accomplish this task, I will be qualified for a promotion! Not just any promotion, but a Kingdom-Oriented position! So now I don't have to worry about being ill-prepared when I minister to God's people on this level. I don't have to worry about people wondering why I'm the right person to give them counsel or spiritual advice in my specialized areas, or why I'm the person who God sent for the specific tasks. All I have to do is give them my resume! My resume is solid not only physically, but spiritually as well.My resume speaks for itself. All of my "should have been dead or crazy" experiences birthed the anointed fire within me. I have experienced and overcome sexual abuse, physical and emotional abuse, nervous breakdowns, severe mind battles, PTSD, incurable medical illnesses, teen pregnancy, STDs, family drug abuse, vast marital storms, desertion, ridicule, and the list goes on. I also have the education and skills that come along with overcoming those things as well.

So, think about it. It is during those times when you experience the tornados and all other kinds of catastrophes in your life that God is building your spiritual resume.

Allow him to build a resume that overflows with high accomplishments, a prestigious spiritual education, and many challenging experiences that illustrate your endurance! It will greatly benefit you. Always remember: "The righteous person faces many troubles, but the Lord comes to the rescue each time" (Psalm 34:19 NLT). You will come out victoriously if you hold on and believe!

~

Victims of sexual assault are:

26 times more likely to abuse drugs;

13 times more likely to abuse alcohol;

6 times more likely to suffer from PTSD;

4 times more likely to consider suicide;

& 3 times more likely to suffer from depression. [4]

7

Lemons to Lemonade

❧

Prophetically, God told me in these words: "I have called Nioka for a time such as this. Nioka was born for a time such as this. Nioka was slain for a time such as this!" I was called to say to the captive, break free and to help those in darkness to come out! This is my mission. This is my purpose. This is why I was born. I was slain for this! I was slain for you! It was for me, each person reading this book, each woman and girl whose lives I have touched, am currently impacting, and will impact in the future. Why is it so important for you to know this? Everything that I've been through was for this very moment, the amazing moments I'm living now, and for the impact I'm making for God's Kingdom now. God woke me out of my sleep one night to tell me that He called me from the bowels of my mother's womb and mentioned my very name while I was yet in her womb (Isaiah 49:1). He told me that He kept me for a time such as this! It's so crucial for you to grasp the magnitude of the power of this because just like I was slain and kept for a reason, you too, have been or will be slain and kept for your life's purpose! You see, purpose is the most powerful and effective route of turning your lemons into lemonade. Purpose is your vehicle that gets you from victim to victor. Purpose increases your motivation and automatically provides you with fuel to get through by any means necessary. You were born with purpose. You don't have to go far to find it; it's already within you. I am able to minister to women and girls who have psychological issues such as depression, suicidal thoughts, severe anxiety, and mental attacks. I have helped numerous women and girls rise above these circumstances. I told you I was slain for this! You too, were slain for some greater purpose. You too, were born, for a greater purpose. **Your past is not your purpose; it's your key to activating your purpose.**

God wants me to tell my sisters; my divas; His daughters; that it won't always be like this. There are two steps that God gave me that empowered me to turn my life's lemons into lemonade. I want to share those tools with you.

Lemons to Lemonade Step #1
Accept God's Grace

In order to accept God's grace, you must first understand some things about God and how His love reaches beyond all mistakes and all blemishes. Seek a relationship with God through prayer and Bible reading. Here, you will find peace as God's grace begins to rest upon you. God said His grace is sufficient for you and His power is made perfect in your weakness (II Corinthians 12:9). Seek to know God because to know God is to know love. To know God is to know peace. To know God is to know grace! There are a lot of ways to explain God's grace. The way

I see it is that **grace is God's favor to the rescue. Grace is His favor toward your unfavorable circumstances.** When we've made a devastating mistake, been victimized in some way, or the demands of life have bogged us down to the ground, we are in need of being rescued. No matter the case, when we are in a rut, God's favor shows up to liberate us—even when we least deserve it. Now that's what you call grace!

When I was experiencing all the illnesses with PTSD, severe anxiety disorder, and narcolepsy, I was also sick in my body in so many other ways. At one point in time, I was on eleven different medications suffering from *daily* migraine headaches... flu here, sinusitis there, and more. All of the stress, PTSD, and anxiety weakened my immune system.

On top of all of that, I failed to realize that I had taken on my father's shame and sins. I was keeping his sins a secret and harboring his shame as my own.

I remember being *right* in the middle of losing my mind.

I was getting in the tub with my clothes on, forgetting everything, unable to construct a complete sentence, overly emotional, paranoid, unable to cope with the smallest things, having bowel movements literally every hour, trembling nonstop, unable to sleep, unexplainably anxious, hearing voices, incapable of turning off my racing thoughts, experiencing feelings of death, and more. I was completely distant from my current world.

It was like I was in my body without my mind.

I remember having to force myself to pray to God.

And when I did, His grace was sufficient for my very hour. God told me to find a therapist and He led me to the perfect Christian counselor who specializes in sexual abuse. Many people miss out on recognizing God's grace because they don't understand God's love for us.

God wanted me to heal more than I did.

We neglect to seek the help and we neglect to receive the help because no matter how damaged we are; no matter how much we've messed up; no matter how low we have gotten; we fail to understand that God *still* sees the best in us! We fail to grasp God's love and grace. Even when we think we don't deserve better, God still wants what's best for us. So, He extends grace to us. It is up to us to accept His grace.

This is my prayer for you:
> And I pray that you will be rooted and established in love, may have the power... to grasp how wide and long and high and deep is the love of Christ, and to know this love that surpasses knowledge—that you may be filled to the measure of all the fullness of God. Ephesians 3:17-19 NIV

The trials I had gone through (especially with my daddy) made me sometimes feel unlovable. When I grasped how long, how wide, and how high God's love reached, I was able to accept the grace.

When I could not function at work because of the fact that my nerves were unstable, God told me very clearly to quit my job as a high school teacher. I will never forget that evening during prayer. Of course, I knew for a fact that my body and mind could not take an ounce more of pressure.

However, some part of me felt like I didn't deserve to take time for me.

I said, "But God, it's the middle of the school year! I can't just quit. I'm on a teacher's contract."

God said again to me, "Leave your job." I could sense that

this instruction to leave my teaching career was not temporary, so I then said, "But God, I did all that schooling to receive two degrees and now you just want me to leave?" God replied, "I have a greater purpose for you." Whew! This still gives me chills!

On top of that, I could feel God extending His grace to give me the break that my body and mind required. God wanted me to rest. Even more so, God wanted me to *heal* from all the wounds of my past. God knew that this had to be done before I could step into my greater purpose that I'm now walking in. So, I accepted God's grace and quit my dependable teaching job. That meant my husband would be the sole financial provider for our house. This was such a great leap of faith for us. But because I accepted God's grace and quit my job, my husband received a promotion on his job the very next week!

This promotion doubled his salary plus my salary! Wow! God wants the very best for us if we would only grasp Ephesians 3:17-19. He wants us to take the step of faith and accept His grace before we are able to move on to the next steps.

The prosperous blessings didn't stop there! God continued to bless my husband in his career to the point of making a multiple six figure income! Within a moment's time, my husband was making more in a month than I made in an *entire year!* Here I was at home, not working, and we were living in abundance! We didn't have to want for anything! It's all because I accepted God's grace to leave work to heal. Before then, my life was so hectic that I literally did not have the time to focus on myself, my health, or my healing. Once I accepted God's grace to stay home and heal, money was never an issue again. We began to live in abundance and an overflow every day and in every single area of our lives.

The first step in turning your lemons into lemonade is acknowledging God's grace and accepting it!

Another time I accepted God's grace was when I was pregnant with my son at age seventeen. I felt so guilty and ashamed for getting pregnant as a teenager. Quite contrary to my father, my mother has the most loving and giving heart in the world. When she found out I was pregnant, she took me in her arms and showed me nothing but love. She never once treated me differently and always assured me through prayer and rocking me in her arms: "All is well, daughter." She wanted so badly to endure the pain for me. When I thought I had to miss prom, my mother encouraged me to go. With tears rolling down my face, I cried, "We have no money. I cannot fit into a dress. Prom is April 10, 2004 and my due date is April 28, 2004. There is no way!" After thinking it over, my mom took me to a local formal gown shop. I found a dress that was twelve sizes bigger than my number size. It was the only dress that I could fit (and the most expensive). I remember giving up because of the price tag. The next thing I knew, my mother took the dress to the counter, literally signed over her *entire* paycheck to the storeowner, and we walked away with the dress. The baby had completely taken over my teenage body. Although I felt so fat and ugly in that dress, my mother looked at me and told me how beautiful I was. My mother was the only one that seemed to love me at that time. At least, that's how I felt.

Even within all the amazing love my mother showed me, I felt alone. I felt guilty and pathetic. I did not feel like I deserved to be loved because of what I had done. I was so depressed. I had no friends and no date at prom, but I was there hoping and praying my water wouldn't break. I went to prom with a baby in my belly and graduated high school with a baby in my arms.

As years went on and I still carried the heaviness of the guilt on my shoulders, I finally broke down and cried out to God. This is when God showed me that He was extending grace to me the entire time, but I failed to realize it!

On the one hand, I had this father who was so cruel to me.

But on the other hand, I had this mother who was such an angel to me! We must be careful not to allow our brutal circumstances to blind us from seeing the hand of God's grace. God extended grace to me through the unconditional, selfless, amazing love that my mother gave me. My mother even offered to keep my newborn baby so that I could go off to college. Because I finally recognized that this was God's grace; His favor to my rescue; His favor to my *unfavorable* circumstances, I accepted it. I moved two hours away to live in a college dormitory while my baby was not even yet four months old.

> *Sometimes, we focus so much on the noise of the storms in our lives, that we can't even recognize the whispers of the grace in our lives.*

It was one of the hardest things I ever had to do in my life. However, I knew in my spirit that it was God's grace cheering me on and giving me the push to conquer what seemed unconquerable. I knew in my spirit that this was God's grace giving me a second chance at making something great out of my life. I felt it all in my bones that this was God's grace empowering me to defy everything that statistics claimed I would be.

I forgave myself and God healed me from the shame of my teenage pregnancy. I accepted God's grace that gave me the green light to reverse every statistic that had attached itself to my life and my destiny.

Statistics said that because of my teen pregnancy, I would be amongst the 40% of black girls that fail to graduate each year,[1] but grace whispered, "That is a lie!"

Statistics said that I would be one of the 52% of African-American women who have a difficult time paying monthly utility bills,[2] but grace whispered, "That is a lie!"

Statistics said that my children would be amongst the 55% of black kids who live in a single parent household,[3] but grace whispered, "That is a lie!"

Statistics said I would be one of the African-American women who represent 33% of the women on welfare, but grace whispered,[4] "That is a lie!"

Statistics said that because I was sexually abused, I would be a drug addict, alcoholic, prostitute, or promiscuous, but grace whispered,[5] "That is a lie!"

Statistics said I would be just another number, but grace whispered, "That is a lie!"

How is God trying to extend grace to you? How is God trying to shower you with favor during your unfavorable circumstance? How is God's favor trying to rescue the lemons (trials) in your life? If you focus too much on your lemons, they will speak so loudly that you cannot recognize God's grace. Many times, God's grace comes as a gentle whisper.

Elijah was one of God's prophets who had just accomplished two huge victories by defeating the prophets of Baal and accomplishing the answered prayer for rain. However, after these great conquering events, his life was threatened and people were out to kill him. He grew very weary. He had just fought perhaps the biggest battle of his life and the demands of his life had bogged him down. Even in light of his victory, he grew extremely discouraged and felt so heavily defeated that he went and sat under a Juniper tree and asked to die. But God sent an angel to provide food for Elijah and encourage him to rest and eat. Here Elijah was feeling defeated and depressed, and in need of being rescued. So, God extended grace by sending his very own angel to encourage him to rest his body and mind and to ensure him that God's purpose for his life was not over. His circumstances of someone out to kill him were indeed unfavorable, but God sent his very own angels to extend favor within his unfavorable circumstances. Moreover, God informed Elijah of the next steps to take to ensure continual victory and to rise above the circumstances.

Elijah looked for God to speak to him in the loud storm, but God didn't speak through it. Elijah looked for God to speak through the earthquake, but God was not in the earthquake. Elijah looked for God to speak through the fire, but God was not in the fire. Suddenly, after all the intense occurrences, and all was quiet, God spoke to Elijah in a gentle whisper (1 Kings 19:12 NIV). Sometimes, we focus so much on the noise of the storms in our lives, that we can't even recognize the whispers of the grace in our lives. Don't allow the storms of your life to speak so loudly that they drown out the whispers of God's grace! My Diva sister, God's grace is in the whispers! Listen and accept.

Lemons to Lemonade Step #2
Find a New Focus of Inspiration

It's so much easier to focus on things that are constantly before us. Whatever we keep thinking about or focusing on gets magnified. A lot of people say, "Well, I'm focusing on my problems because they're here and they are not going anywhere." I am not telling you to pretend that they are not there because your trials are very much real.

Denial won't help.

I'm merely telling you to find a new focus, but not just any new focus. You must find a focus that motivates or inspires you; something that gets you pumped and keeps you moving.

Find something that you can look forward to.

Whatever is directly before you is what you will be drawn to. Whatever is at the center of your view is what you will focus on. It's what you will work toward. When your trials are in your center view, they become your focal point. A focal point is the center of interest. By focusing on your trials, they become a part of your daily routine and activity. When you focus on your inspiration, it then becomes your daily routine and activity.

So what do you do with your lemons—these trials that are huge, debilitating, and ever so raging before you?

Should you try to force them into a bottle when there's no bottle large enough to fit them? Should you bury them with false happiness and fictitious smiles on your face? Should you attempt to put off your problems until tomorrow and the next day until they suddenly explode at once? Absolutely not. None of this is healthy.

This is how you accomplish step two of turning lemons into lemonade: You acknowledge that the trial is there and real.

You tell the truth! You say, "This battle is huge and it feels too much for me to bear." But you first say it to the Lord. Don't speak it out all carelessly into the atmosphere and allow Satan's angels to grab it. Because when you do that with no power from God behind it, you allow Satan to fester on that trial like a sore. You allow him and his demons to magnify the issues because you didn't speak any word or truth with it.

Instead, say to God, "Lord, my children's father left me with all of these responsibilities and I don't know how I'm going to keep the lights on. My family member is sick and my job has cut my hours. My rent has increased and my car is about to give out on me. Lord, this seems too much to bear. But nevertheless, even though I don't see it, I trust your word that says that you'll never forsake me. You'll never let my kids go begging for bread. You will supply all my needs according to your riches in glory."

There's mighty power behind that! Ms. Diva, you must realize that everything is spiritual! Yes, everything! When you speak, speak it so that God's angels can pick up your words and bless your circumstances, not to where Satan's angels (demons) can pick up your words and curse your circumstances.

So, yes, you acknowledge the truth and how difficult and burdensome your trials are. You speak it to God and not vainly into the atmosphere. You then find a biblical word that matches your situation and pray to God and claim the victory.

This is a matter of using the power and authority that God has given us over every situation. "Behold, I give unto you power to tread on serpents and scorpions, and power over all the power of the enemy, and nothing shall by any means harm you" (Luke 10:19). You must believe this and utilize the power that God has given you over the enemy and your circumstances.

Now, once you acknowledge the truth of your trial and the severity of it, pray to God and speak the word over your situations. **Leave it alone** while you focus on something that inspires you.

Yes, your trial is still there, but so is your faith, and so is God. You must be confident that God is working on it. Continue to pray and meditate on the word each day while simultaneously focusing on your mode of inspiration. The powerful thing about putting faith into action is that it provides a bridge to walk over troubled water. The troubled water is there, but your faith grants protection from the danger while also providing a path to the next destination. "The name of the Lord is a strong tower. The righteous run into and is safe" (Proverbs 18:10).

There are two reasons that you must find something to focus on **even when your battles are not yet resolved.**

The *first* reason is because focusing solely on your battles will utterly consume you!

The *second* reason is that in the meantime while your battles are being resolved, you will be moving forward instead of being stuck and stagnant.

I remember telling my mother, "Mommy, every time I try move forward, something horrible happens in my life and I never get to do what I set out to do." My spiritually strong mother (who is an evangelist and prophetic intercessor) said, "Darling, trials will always be there. The enemy doesn't want you to move forward, so he sends distractions. But you have to press your way through even in the midst of pain and discouragement, because that's how your blessings will be birthed. That's where the power will come from."

It all made sense to me after she said that.

I would have continued to have been setback if I didn't push through. The moment we get out of one battle, another one comes. While we're in that battle, another one is awaiting soon. Just like Job in the Bible.

God never promised us that we won't have trials. He said to be of good cheer because every trial that we endure, Jesus overcame each one on the cross. There is power in His resurrection that we *all* have access to. We have confidence in proclaiming the word of God over our situations that *this too shall pass.*

While the storms are raging in your life, pray, proclaim, and work toward that goal you've always dreamed of. Explore that talent that you've hidden. Pursue that project that you've made excuses for. Allow your fiery trials to become the fuel for your blessings. *Allow your trials to inspire you instead of allowing them to devour you.*

Instead of allowing my pain to defeat me, I allowed my pain to inspire me.

I knew where I came from.

I knew that I had a baby before graduating high school.

I knew that no one in my family had graduated college with a bachelor's degree.

However, I was destined to take all of the adversities and use them to make me better.

Instead of settling and staying at a standstill in life, I prayed about it. I told God I wanted to go to college.

It was extremely hard to work, go to college full-time, and tend to a family with only one car and a minimum wage income. However, I was inspired and found a new focus! Instead of focusing on my calamitous circumstances, I focused on something that inspired me. I took my life's lemons and made lemonade.

Did my trials disappear?

No, not immediately.

I had to work through my trials of being a teenage mom in school, a very young lady still very much dealing with the abuse of her father, the violence within her family, the poverty-stricken background, and so much more. I acknowledged (not out loud-in vain, or in my head-in vain) to God in prayer that this was difficult. I even cried and told him how I felt like I wasn't going to make it. I told him how I felt like this was too much to bear and how I wanted to quit.

But I also told God that I knew He was with me. I told him my desires and proclaimed the scripture that says God would

"Give me the desires of my heart if I delight myself in Him". It was extremely difficult, but I stood on faith and I stood on God's word while focusing on what inspired me. Over time, things definitely got better, but it was a process. If I had just laid down while passively focusing on my trials, it would have been a double loss for me and a win-win for Satan. I would have gone through the overwhelming trials; plus, I would have lost the chance to receive three college degrees and so much more. I am now a Marriage and Family Therapist/Licensed Clinical Christian Counselor, and a Board Certified Christian Life Coach! I graduated college with a bachelor's degree (a four year degree) in only three years. At the time of graduation, I had not one, but two children with my husband. I then graduated three years later with a third child and a second college degree—a Master's Degree. After numerous tribulations and three kids later, I earned my Doctorate in Christian Counseling!

I'm so amazed at God's glory!

All that I've been through, this was not supposed to be my story! If I did it, imagine what you can do through God!

I have been happily and successfully married to the man of my dreams for over thirteen years. My husband is not just a person I'm married to. He is my best friend. He protects me, assures me of my worth and my beauty, greatly provides for our family, and cherishes me beyond measure. Most importantly, he loves me like Christ loves the church and would give up his life for me. We have a marriage that ministers to so many young adults today. We encourage and bless so many other people in their relationships, young and old, because of the blessings and favor on our marriage. We are called power couple everywhere we go. My husband and I are best friends.

We cry together, laugh together, pray together, play together, work together, and grow together.

But God already knew that we would be this influential power couple. It was part of his design for us from the beginning. God already has amazing things in His design for your life as well. It's a process that you must pass through and over. My husband and I built our own house from the ground up and became homeowners at the age of twenty-five. I am the CEO of J. Kenkade Publishing, a

The powerful thing about putting faith into action is that it provides a bridge to walk over troubled water.

successful book publishing company that is constantly on the rise. I am President of a Non-Profit Organization that I founded called "Our Daughters Keeper" where we empower at-risk teenage girls through several intervention tools. I have my own Life Coach and Christian Counseling Practice. I travel around speaking to other women and girls to inspire and empower them. My husband is an incredibly successful businessman and is also very active in the ministry. Our kids are all amazing, fun, well-mannered, talented, beautiful kids who excel in their academics. My husband and I are very financially blessed and our cup runs over! I tell you this to boast in God *alone* on how He can take two people from impoverished homes and grace them with a life that they only heard about on television. But I had to accept God's grace and transfer my focus of inspiration.

I had to find something to inspire me. The possibility of gaining a college degree is what inspired me! It helped me to stop focusing on my pain and my past and start focusing on God and my desire to be successful. Therefore, I put everything I had into school. Everything! I chose not to focus on destructive things that are so easily to be pulled into such as promiscuity, drugs, alcohol, club hopping, etc. In a sense, school was my drug. I had to put all my energy into my faith in God and my college courses, or I would not be where I am today.

You must be inspired by your trials. What lemons has life given you? How can you turn those lemons into lemonade? Remember to pray consistently and have faith in God to assist you. Then, find something positive that can inspire you or motivate you. God should be your first focus. Isaiah 26:3 says, "God will keep you in perfect peace if you keep your mind stayed on him." A scripture that carried me through my trials during that time was Romans 8:28. Ask God to give you a scripture to help carry you through whatever trials you experience.

~

Because I recognized and accepted God's grace, found a new focus of inspiration, and walked by faith, God turned me from victim to victor! I am no longer a victim of my life's lemons. God gave me more than double for my trouble and turned my lemons into lemonade through the grace of God.

I knew what statistics said about my future.

But God intervened and did not let any of this be so!

God says in exchange for our shame, He will give us a double portion of honor, prosperity, and everlasting joy (see Isaiah 61:7). I'm a witness that God will completely take away your shame and cause you to prosper and be elevated in the midst of your enemies and in the face of adversity.

My Diva sister, do not be dismayed by the tornadoes and other storms in your life, but be assured that God will give you double for your trouble.

When you surrender all to God and allow Him to be the author of your life, He will rewrite your story. Then, He will take those chapters in your life that the devil meant for your harm and He will perfect your story! God is the greatest author! Allow God to rewrite your story and perfect your story.

He is able to take every lemon in your life and turn it into lemonade. In fact, God is able to not only turn your lemons into lemonade, He is also able to make sure you never run out of lemonade! That's right! God promises us that whoever drinks from the water that *He* gives will never be thirsty again (John 4:14). You will never run out of your blessings, prosperity, joy, and peace if you lean and depend on God. Learn to take the word of God and use it against the devil. Use God's word against the lemons Satan has thrown at you. God's word (the Bible) is your sword against Satan. Fight Satan with prayer and the word of God and you will win!

8

Breaking the Chains Of Strongholds

A lthough I had accepted God's grace regarding my past and had found a new focus of inspiration, I still struggled in my spirit because there were still some unresolved issues that I hadn't visited. I was college educated, financially secure, and very successful; yet, I sat on the floor of my bedroom crying heavy tears to my husband one night. I was in so much pain that it honestly felt like my heart was missing out of my chest. For months, I literally walked around feeling like my heart was not there. So many times, I would place my hand on my chest to feel for a heartbeat and could not even feel my own heartbeat. I knew that it was spiritual and not physical. I was extremely happy within my marriage and my life. I was living in abundance, but I was still empty in some areas of my life. I was blessed. I was favored. Yet and still, I found myself crying at restaurant dining tables. In fact, every time I had a quiet moment, I began to cry and didn't know why. My husband was concerned and so was I. God revealed to me that I was still feeling pain and emptiness from my past with my dad and my childhood upbringing. It is very important that we find a new focus of inspiration as instructed in the last chapter; however, we must be careful not to abandon our heart matters.

Be careful not to ignore the screams from the strongholds.

Find a new focus of inspiration, realizing that you must one day revisit your heart matters at some point in order to completely conquer deeply buried issues.

Whether subtle or severe, we all have, will have, or have previously had strongholds in our lives.

Someone's stronghold may be drug usage or a sexual addiction. Others may have strongholds in the areas of poverty, illnesses, finances, their career, fear, an abusive relationship, failed relationships, sexual abuse, abandonment, depression, unforgiveness, etc. You must identify and warfare against your strongholds.

Strongholds are wrong thinking patterns that have been strongly molded into our minds and are powerfully dominated by Satan. If you look in the dictionary, it will also tell you that strongholds are forts. A fort is "a strong or fortified place; occupied only by troops and surrounded with such works as a ditch…where soldiers live."

Allow me to put it in these words: *a stronghold is a place in your mind that is orchestrated by Satan, armed by his demons, and designed to manipulate the way you think and perceive things.* Whenever there is an army post, it is almost impossible to get through an army of soldiers. It would take a lot of work and a lot of weapons; in this case…spiritual weapons.

A stronghold is a place where Satan's soldiers reside and they will protect their territory at any cost, refusing to leave. Because

Satan and his demons are spiritual, the only way to fight Satan's army is with another spiritual army, one mightier than Satan. That is God and God's angels. Strongholds are spiritual and cannot be done away with by a person's physical actions.

The following scriptures were the basis for the vision of this book:

> "Although we walk in the flesh, we do not war according to the flesh. The weapons of our warfare are not carnal, but mighty through God, to the pulling down of strongholds, casting down imaginations, and every high thing that exalts itself against the knowledge of God, and bringing into captivity every thought to the obedience of Christ" (II Corinthians 10:3-5).

Our Weapons Against our Battles are Spiritual, Not Physical

The weapons of our warfare are not carnal, but mighty through God, to the pulling down of strongholds. (verse 4)

Too often, we still try to fight our situations with our physical strength and physical weapons. Physical weapons cannot defeat a spiritual army; only spiritual weapons can do that. The scriptures above tell us that our weapons are not carnal (not worldly; not humanly). Our weapons are *spiritual* (through God) because God is a spirit. Our weapons are the knowledge and word of God, our faith, and our prayers. That's what you must fight with! In the introduction, I mentioned that Satan begins planting several small seeds in our minds and lives when we are little children. The stuff we saw, heard, witnessed, and experienced all contribute to the reasons we do things later on in our lives. It's one way that wrong thinking patterns (also known as strongholds) enter into our minds. The issue is that we don't realize that what happened twenty years ago has created chaos in our lives today. Satan plants those seeds in our minds as a child, so that by the time we become adults, the small seeds grow into plants of defeat. The things people around us wore led us to believe that it's okay to dress the way we dress.

Ever wonder why women and girls tolerate such misuse and disrespect from men?

Much of it has to do with a stronghold because oftentimes, they had mothers, aunts, or sisters whose boyfriends didn't work, but depended on the women to provide. Oftentimes, they watched women around them with husbands and boyfriends who repeatedly cheated because it was acceptable. They witnessed these women's husbands or boyfriends call them all kinds of degrading names, get drunk all the time, then come back and apologize only to do it over again.

They observed women within their families go to work all day, do all the cooking, cleaning, and tending to the kids while the man laid around the house playing video games or hanging out with his friends all times of the day and night.

Many women that you see today were actually once girls who told themselves, "Oh no! I will not have a man like that. I will not put up with that."

However, gradually, with no verbal permission, Satan and his army created a place (a stronghold) within the thoughts of the little girl's head who observed all of that.

He whispered to her subconscious, "This is the type of man to attract when you get older. This is what to look forward to.

This is all you know. This is the type of man in your future."

Over time, the little girl became a woman who has unknowingly had this subtle stronghold lying dormant within her. No matter how much she tries to steer clear of those male types, the stronghold reels her right back into their arms. She constantly attracts these same types of men and doesn't know why.

Something keeps pulling her there and keeping her there even when she wants out! This is a stronghold armed by Satan and his soldiers.

The same thing goes for the level of accomplishment in our lives. Many women today who are on welfare, in minimum wage jobs, or in dead-end jobs may have once been little girls who dreamed to be a nurse, doctor, teacher, or singer. However, something happened along the lines that opened the door for Satan and his army of demons to alter the way of thinking within the little girl or woman.

Maybe the stronghold entered when she looked around her family and neighborhood and saw that no one was successful; everyone struggled to even pay utility bills. Maybe the stronghold was placed when the girl was a teenager and she was sexually abused. In the midst of the abuse, her way of thinking changed to not being good enough for any great level of success.

Or perhaps, she was neglected by her mom or dad, and a stronghold created a sense of instability in her life to where she's all over the place; never consistent with anything.

Whatever the event, something occurred that gradually altered and damaged her way of thinking to the point to where she cannot see herself or her life the way God sees her. And even when she tries so hard to get ahead—when she tries so hard not to repeat the same errors, something (the stronghold) draws her back and won't let go, thrusting her into a cycle of dead end, unsatisfying jobs.

Take heed. **Whenever you see a vicious cycle that keeps repeating itself in your life, more than likely, it's a stronghold.**

Satan is so crafty that he enforces strongholds in your life over several months and years so that you won't even notice your thought patterns changing or being damaged. This way, by the time you realize it, you'll be so confused as to why you do what you do, why you allow what you allow, and why you just can't get it right. **Strongholds will leave you with a thousand questions and no direction.** Strongholds are so difficult to break because the army of Satan is guarding them and protecting their territory inside of your mind.

As the scripture says, the *only* way to tackle this army of Satan is with the army of God. God is a spirit (of good), but Satan is also a spirit (of evil). You cannot fight a spirit with natural weapons. Imagine constantly punching a spirit with your fist. Fighting the devil on your own is like fighting the air. You become exhausted, your opponent is unharmed, and your problems are still there.

All of the heartaches, setbacks, depression; all of the failed attempts to move ahead in life, failed attempts to make a relationship work, to stop drinking, to stop having premarital sex; the failed attempts to stay away from useless men and tired relationships, continual financial hardships, and the same cycle of continuous dead-end jobs are all tied to strongholds that women try to fight with natural weapons, or their own willpower. The cycles will continue until you use your spiritual weapons of prayer and God's word, and until you rearrange your thought patterns. "Don't copy the behavior and customs of this world, but let God transform you into a new person by changing the way you think" (Romans 12:2 NLT).

God is probably beginning to open your eyes to the strongholds that are keeping you chained as you read this chapter.

Pray the following prayer.

Dear God,

I come to you in the name of Jesus asking that you would for-give me of sins; known and unknown. I realize that there may be some things in my life that are keeping me from the truth. There may have been some moments in my life where Satan entered to damage my thought patterns. I pray that you will open my eyes to see things the way you see them. I pray that you will show me any and all strongholds that Satan has placed within me. I pray that you will give me the tools, wisdom, and diligence to renounce every single stronghold that is keeping me stagnant and keeping me chained. I reject every stronghold by the blood of Jesus. Amen.

So once you are able to identify your own strongholds, you must first take God's word to learn what God says about your situation. God's word tells us that we are free from strongholds; however, we must do our part in making sure that we *stay* free from strongholds (Galatians 5:1).

Evaluate your strongholds, and use the weapons of the Holy Spirit, God's Holy word, prayer, and faith to fight the army of Satan's angels. God plus you equals victory every time! When you go against Satan alone, you are outnumbered! Period. When you go against Satan and his army with God and God's army, you win! Period.

A warfare is a fight against a great army. The weapons of your *warfare* are not physical, but Godly and will enormously pull down every stronghold that has led to the chains on your life!

Once you identify the strongholds against your life, you cannot only pray two or three times. The scripture says "the weapons of our *warfare*" are not carnal. A warfare is a fight!

Yes, God's children must fight!

Whether we like it or not, we're already in a fight anyway.

Satan is relentlessly fighting us all. Every day.

The problem is that most people don't fight him back.

Instead, we fight people, ourselves, and things.

You must fight the source, which is Satan, but not with worldly weapons (Ephesians 6:12). Fight by continuously praying. Fight by continuously speaking God's word against Satan. Fight by continuing to put your faith in action through your everyday walk with God. "Blessed be the Lord my strength, which teacheth my hands to war, and my fingers to fight" (Psalm 144:1).

As a coping mechanism, I allowed Satan to convince me that holding on to the toxic relationship with my daddy was the way to stay sane. In my mind, I thought that if that relationship died, I would not survive. The absolute *worst* thing that could have happened to me at that time was losing the hope for the little seven year old girl whose daddy walked out of her life for six years and took her self-confidence and self-worth with him. Can you see how this is all spiritual?

Through the stronghold, that little seven-year-old girl had convinced herself and convinced me that in order to regain her self-worth, confidence, and voice, she'd have to hold on to her daddy at any cost! Even in the midst of it killing her! This was an imagination—an argument from Satan that had exalted itself against the knowledge of God.

Losing my daddy meant killing all hope for that little girl. Being attached to my daddy meant being attached to the seven-year-old Nioka. Being attached to my daddy meant keeping the seven-year-old girl alive. It meant keeping the door open for her to get her daddy back.

However, this desire to be attached to something that was so toxic to me and my health is the clearest sign of a stronghold. My way of thinking was that my healing was attached to my daddy. What a clever way for the enemy to blind me! Look at how he carefully started planting these seeds into my imagination when I was such a little girl. Even after the incestuous sexual abuse, I continued to be hurt time after time by my father. In my mind, that was the way to heal the seven-year-old girl. The stronghold was so potent that my attachment to my daddy almost killed me! Literally!

~

Incest is more damaging than sexual abuse by a stranger due to the added violation of the victim's trust for the family member. [1]

Detach & Reattach

Suddenly one day, I heard God tell me to cut all ties with my father for the time being. God told me it was time to let it all go. He said it was time to face it head on. God was also telling me that it was finally time to tell my story.

God told me to no longer cover or hide my daddy's secret.

This is when I discovered that the sexual abuse (the incest) wasn't my secret to keep or my shame to bear.

It was *his* shame. *His* secret. Research shows that on average, it takes a person *twelve entire years* to disclose that they were sexually abused as a child. [2]

I'm a witness.

I was in those numbers!

It's just that traumatic!

But I have learned that the longer we keep quiet, the longer Satan gets to hide—the stronger the demons become—and the more power the abuser keeps over us.

We as women and girls have to stop allowing Satan to hide behind our pain! *We've got to stop protecting the secrets and shame of our abusers at the expense of our pain!*

Your abuser may not be a sexual abuse incident or even a person. Maybe your abuser is an illness, guilt and depression from an abortion or a mistake you made, a sexual addiction, wrong choices, reoccurring bad relationships, constant dead-end jobs, or some other bad habit.

Either way, you must detach yourself from it and expose Satan because he wants to stay hidden so that you won't know truth. Reattach yourself to God as your main source!

I knew God was preparing me for ministry in this area. Everything in me was aware that this would be one of the most trying tests of my life. With the advice of my therapist, I wrote a letter to my mom and told her. Now, it was time to write my father and end my relationship with him.

Listen to me when I say this was the *absolute* hardest thing I have ever had to do in my entire life! It literally felt like a death. I mourned so badly. It took me weeks to finally do as God had told me to do because the stronghold was so powerful! I hurt all inside of my body.

I felt like death!

I felt like the little girl was dying because at the time, it felt like there was no more hope for the little girl. The stronghold said that if I detached myself from my daddy, I was saying goodbye to that little girl forever. Saying goodbye to her meant she had been worthless all along, which is what she was most afraid of. The essence of why she held on to the toxic relationship with her father was to validate her worth. Now, it felt all in vain and she was worthless, hopeless, and desolate. Pulling down strongholds may require you to let go of something that you have held on to so closely. You may have to detach yourself

We as women and girls have to stop allowing Satan to hide behind our pain!

from whatever was tied to the stronghold. Unfortunately, mine just happened to be my relationship with my daddy. It may feel like a death, but in the end, it will birth so much life, freedom, victory, and peace. Just be sure that after you detach from that source, you *re*attach yourself to God!

At first, I didn't understand why it was so hard to cut all ties with my daddy. Of course, it was the common question about, "Do you really write your own biological father out of your life? Do people really do that?"

But most importantly and more severely, it was the aching feeling of terminating a relationship that I had held on to for so long. I had put all my hope and worth into that relationship. It was the heart wrenching pain of feeling like your biggest dream you craved for was killed. No matter how much pain he had caused me, how much shame and torment his actions had brought me, or how the relationship with him was killing me, I had held on to the hopes of one day having the same relationship I had with him when I was five and six years old.

I know. It sounds absurd to think that my grown self would ever have the same kind of father-daughter relationship I had as a little girl. It sounds even sillier to think that this relationship would be possible after he had sexually abused me! But it's true. Those were my thought patterns (hence, strongholds). The actions that strongholds cause sometimes only make sense in the eyes of the victim.

We can refer to the women who continue to run to the men who abuse or misuse them. To us, it seems stupid! To that woman, it makes sense to go back to him because she's in need of something that she feels he can offer; she's holding on to the one or two times that he actually treated her right; or she's simply holding on to the hopes of the relationship that they once had or that she once witnessed.

Maybe, she too, is trying to fill a void for the little girl in her that yearns for some male validation.

The list of reasons goes on and on. However, the fact is that this woman is being dominated by a stronghold; a place in her mind that is orchestrated by Satan, armed by his demons, and is manipulating the way she thinks and perceives things.

So, because my obligations to my kids began to suffer, because my health was immensely threatened, and because I would get in more trouble if I didn't obey God, I wrote my daddy a letter.

I wasn't strong enough to talk to him face to face at the time because at this time, I was still fainting to the ground and trembling all over my body at the sight of him (PTSD). I sent the letter "certified" mail so that I could receive a signature and notification when he received it.

In the letter, I informed my daddy of every hurtful thing he had done to me. I explained that my turmoil exceeded beyond the sexual abuse. The threats, violence, and emotional abuse severely injured me just as well. I told my daddy how he had snatched away my self-worth, confidence, peace, and even my voice. I told him how he had instilled a type of fear in me where I was afraid to be myself, afraid to sleep at night, and afraid to wake up and breathe. I told him how everything that he had taken from me was what I needed for my ministry. I let him know that I was detaching myself from depending on him as a source in order to depend on God as my source. I advised him I was taking back my power and my voice. I told him that I loved him, I forgave him, but could not ever talk to him again until I healed and until God said so.

Casting down imaginations and every high thing
that exalts itself against the knowledge of God. (verse 5a)

I had to cast down the imagination that holding on to my daddy and our tumultuous relationship would heal the little girl in me. That was Satan working against the knowledge of God. Through prayer and the Holy Spirit, I realized that this imagination (this high thing, this stronghold) had exalted itself against the knowledge of God. In a way, the demonic stronghold told me to "save the little girl" even if it meant killing myself.

How deceitful!

The stronghold had blinded me so terribly that I couldn't see that if I died as a result of the turmoil I was putting my body through, that little girl would also die because she was a part of *me.*

Think about it.

In what ways has Satan convinced you to do things that are actually detrimental to your body or destructive to your life?

How have the strongholds in your life hindered you from moving forward in life?

Satan's plan is always to *kill,* steal, and destroy. God's plan is for you to live and live more abundantly (John 10:10).

His plan was to kill me by convincing me to save that little girl. His ultimate plan was to steal my peace and destroy my purpose and destiny. However, we must understand that Satan is a defeated foe! He was defeated at the cross.

This is why the scriptures (II Corinthians 10:3-5) are so important to your victory! It tells us to cast down everything that exalts itself against the knowledge of God.

I had to cast down this lie that Satan fed me about holding on to something that was killing me in order to save something that was starving in me.

Are you trying to feed something that's starving within you at the cost of your wellbeing?

Are you trying to keep something alive that is killing you?

Are you holding on to something or someone that's impacting your peace, joy, and destiny?

Choose today to cast down those imaginations and lies that are against the truth of God.

Bring Every Thought Captive

And bringing into captivity every thought to the obedience of Christ
(verse 5b)

Basically, we must arrest the thoughts from the stronghold and command them to obey the thoughts of God. Once we denounce the stronghold and cast down imaginations and every high thing that exalts itself against God, we must lastly take the thoughts that Satan has placed in our minds and make them all match the thoughts of God. What does God and His word say about it? The sexual abuse isn't the only trauma I wrestled with from my childhood. If you can recall, I was severely impacted by all of the violence within my home. During the majority of my childhood, I witnessed men physically abuse my sister and my mother. We ran from bullets flying through our house. I lived in houses where doors had been broken in and kicked down. I watched bloody, fatal fights amongst my own siblings and other family members. I shivered at the behavior of an alcoholic and drug-addicted father. I suffered my father violently threatening me and continuously endangering my life.

My life was a series of emergency situations with my brothers and close family members. There was always someone in my family yelling something like:

Run! Hide! There's the police!

He's about to shoot him!

Go catch him ma'! He got a gun.

Oh God. Please no!

He's jumping on that girl! Oh my God!

Call 911!

Hurry. We have to get him/her to the hospital.

He's into it with those boys! They got guns!

Something bad is happening! Pray right now! Bye!

I was startled repeatedly throughout my childhood. I was never a participant of any of this, but because I was an observer of all of this, I internalized it. Who would've known that this would contribute to my PTSD, severe anxiety disorder, and nervous breakdown many years later? This was all too much on me as a child. It caused me to be unstable as a child and later as an adult. Nonetheless, I made my thoughts obedient to God by continuously speaking the truth aloud.

"Nioka, that was your family in the past. God has given you a new family and a new life. Let go of the old life. Look at the beautiful new life God has given you with your husband and kids. The old life is gone. God has made all things new for you."

My childhood home: unstable; unsafe; violent; sadness; fear
My new home: stable; secure; serene; joyfulness; peace

And when the pain from the little girl in me crept up, I would arrest all the thoughts to make them obey what God said about that little girl and myself.

The stronghold whispered, "Go to your daddy. Risk your heart again. Expose yourself to all of the emotional abuse again. Your daddy is your source. He is where all of your self-worth, validation, happiness, peace, and joy will come from."

The thoughts of God (according to His word) whispered, "God is your daddy! God is your source. God said my peace I leave with you. My peace I give you. The peace I give to you is a peace that man can never give. Therefore, do not worry where it will come from (John 14:27). God created you with worth. Nothing He creates is without worth. He is not *a* source; He is *the* source! You are fearfully and wonderfully made!"

And again,
The thoughts of Satan said, "You will lose your mind if you detach yourself from your daddy as your worth."

But the thoughts of God said, "I will protect you and command my angels to keep you" (Psalm 91:11).

The thoughts of Satan said, "If you write your daddy out of your life like God says, you are going to cause your daddy to have another heart attack and cause him to die."

But the thoughts of God said, "And even if that happens, we know that all things (including my daddy's health status) work together for the good to them that love God who are called according to His purpose" (Romans 8:28).

The thoughts of Satan said, "This is far too much for you to bear Nioka. You are already passing out, nerves are all over the place, and you can barely hold a pencil. You cannot handle this. And it's not going to get any better."

But the thoughts of God said, "I will be with Nioka in trouble. I will deliver her" (Psalm 91:14-15).

~

Do you see how I *commanded* the thoughts of Satan to line up with the thoughts of God? **The only way to overcome the mind of a stronghold is with the mind of Christ.** I arrested those lying thoughts! I brought them all captive and demanded those thoughts to obey God! Each day, you must make it a daily practice to adopt the mind of Christ, not your thoughts or the thoughts of others. Make a list of every lie that Satan has placed in your mind, then research and meditate to see what God says about it. Meditate on it every single day, and speak it with the power God has given you!

Believe that you have broken the chains off your mind and off your life! And when those thoughts (that you now know are lies) come into your mind, cast them down because they are working against the knowledge of God.

Be unbothered by Satan's lies and false imaginations because you have every power to make your mind obey God. I realized that every time the fear from my past crept up, it was the little girl in me; not *me*. The little girl still thought she was alone, worthless, and powerless. Of course, that was a deceitful lying thought pattern that had a stronghold on me. Once I attached myself to God as my source, God revealed something so profound to me. During meditation, He took me back to several special events in my life as a little girl. God showed me how He was present at every award program, every graduation, every spelling bee, every school presentation, and honors banquet. He showed me how He was there cheering me on saying, "Look at my daughter. Look at my baby. I'm so proud of her! That's who I created her to be!"

Wow! This still gives me chills today!

This was the first time I saw God not just as my Father, but as my *Daddy!* This Godly Daddy's love is something I want *every one of my DIVA sisters* to feel and to know! Strongholds will have you thinking that you **need** and cannot do without a man, woman, friend, the club, a drink, sex, or some other person or thing. However, Ms. Diva, I am a living and honest witness that God will be exactly who you need Him to be in every moment if you would just depend on Him as your source! Through my detachment and reattachment process, I was able to see the comparisons between my earthly daddy and my heavenly daddy.

My earthly daddy: imperfect, hurtful, love is defiled, fallible
My heavenly daddy: perfect, healer, pure & undefiled, infallible

During my healing process, I went to a pottery painting venue where I painted a house that represented the new life that God had blessed me with. It represented peace, joy, and redemption because He had redeemed me from the hand of the enemy and from the demons of my past. When I looked at it, I realized that there was no reason to be afraid because there were no gunshots fired through the windows of my house. I didn't have a choice as a little girl, but today, I have a choice of who I can be in my home. The choice to be free! The choice to be *me!* When I looked at the pottery of the house that I painted, I felt safe. I repeated to myself that I was in a safe house now.

There was no man there to molest or abuse me. This new house had come with a protector that God provided for me which was my husband. God and my husband were my protectors. I told the little girl she didn't have to be afraid anymore. Even deeper and more powerful was the revelation that the little girl in me was now safe! The little girl in me was now protected!

This Nioka knows her worth; therefore, the strongholds have been broken—the strongholds were attached to a worthless, voiceless, powerless little girl. That little girl is now a powerful woman full of purpose, life, worth, and a strong and impactful voice! The deceit of Satan said the only way to save the hurt and lost little girl in me was to engage in a relationship while it killed the adult me. However, God knew that in order for me to free and heal the little girl in me while at the same time saving my life was to detach myself from the toxic relationship with my father. So I did.

～

What destructive cycles are being repeated in your life?

What lies and nightmares are your strongholds telling you?

Bring those thoughts captive!

Arrest those thoughts today and make them obey the thoughts of Christ. God tells us to have the *same* mindset as Christ (Philippians 2:5). In order to pull down those strongholds and break away from the chains in your life, you must choose to adopt God's way of thinking! God knew that by me detaching myself from my daddy meant reattaching myself to Him (Jesus). Whereas, I had looked at my daddy my entire life as my source of self-worth and validation, I had to learn to depend solely on God to be my source. This, in turn, not only gave me back my voice, self-worth, and validation, but this also healed the little girl in me and redeemed *me*!

So many women today are looking for that same type of validation in other men, and they continue to be hurt, humiliated, and rejected because something in them longs for self-worth and validation—which was supposed to come from her father, and ultimately comes from God. This internal aching void leads to a stronghold and keeps her bound.

I prayed every day. I cast down the strongholds everyday by saying I don't receive it. I don't receive the unhealthy soul tie. I don't receive the dependence on the toxic relationship. I want no part of it. I rejected the stronghold.

I had to bring every thought captive unto God. I told myself daily that God had given me a new life; a new family. I had to tell myself that God (not my daddy) was the avenue of healing that little girl in me. Over time, my mind was renewed. I had to overrule Satan's word with God's word.

Hurt to Heal

What began as an excruciatingly painful separation from my father allowed me to take time to cry for the little girl in me. Every day, I had to hurt to heal. Every single day, I was in severe pain with the hole in my heart, missing, until it gradually came back little by little. Every day, I cried for hours on the floor for my healing; for my deliverance. And you better believe there were so many days that I'd much rather run from the pain. Like most people, I thought it was better if I didn't *feel*. But the longer we wait, the stronger the stronghold becomes.

So, I chose to *feel* even though all the painful memories and the reality of a toxic, terminating relationship felt like death. Every single day, I prayed against unholy soul ties with my daddy and cast down every stronghold that Satan had built through the means of my daddy. This is what it takes for true deliverance and healing.

Have you cried for the little girl in you?

If you don't cry for the little girl in you, who will?

If you don't tend to the little girl in you, the void and ghost of her past will continue to creep into your life and eat at your peace and joy.

Every time you try to move ahead in certain areas, that stronghold will act as a stumbling block. I had to realize that the little girl in me was acting out in unhealthy ways because she was reaching out. Not only was she reaching out to the ones who hurt her, but she was also reaching out for me! She needed me to cry for her. She needed me to love on her. She needed me to visit with her and give her the time she deserves and to know that she is important, loved, special, beautiful, and worthy. And just maybe, Ms. Diva, there's

୨ଈ
If you don't tend to the little girl in you, the void and ghost of her past will continue to creep into your life and eat at your peace and joy.

a little girl in you who needs you too.It will hurt to visit the past. It will hurt to feel the pain all over again. But as long as you have identified and denounced your strongholds, the enemy has been exposed and you and God can team up and go to war! Sometimes, it takes hurting in order to heal.

No More Chains!

Years before I ever knew I had these strongholds on my life, I awoke from a nap and I heard the voice of God say, "I'm going to purify your pain." I thought to myself, "Huh God? You're going to *purify* my pain?" I remember thinking so hard for so long, "Why in the world would someone's pain need to be *purified?*" I've heard of *healing* someone's pain, but never *purifying* it. That baffled me for years. For one, I didn't know what pain God was referring to. For two, I didn't understand how someone's pain could be purified. Once I began experiencing the traumatic PTSD, severe anxiety, and nervous attacks, the Holy Spirit brought those words of God back to my remembrance. You see, when a woman is sexually abused, her pain is coupled with feelings of uncleanness. From the moment my daddy sexually abused me up until the day I began my healing (about 12 years later), I felt nasty, dirty, worthless, and impure. There were so many times I couldn't even touch or look at my own breasts without detesting them, feeling like they were the dirtiest things on my body. So, when God whispered to me that He was going to purify my pain, He was telling me that He was going to get rid of all the contaminants from the sexual abuse that caused my pain. And He did just that! The contaminants were the embarrassment, shame, and disgust that I felt with my own body in every place that my daddy had so wrongly touched. Today, I love my body. I embrace every beauty and every flaw as a woman and a wife. How amazing is God and His power to break all strongholds and every yoke!

I have a prophetic gift. Many times, God shows me visions and speaks to me through visions. During my healing process; when I was closer to deliverance, God gave me a very powerful vision. As I closed my eyes in meditation unto God and submission to Him as my source in lieu of my daddy, I saw pages of my life flip. On one end of the chapter was this mean, abusive, manipulative father. I saw him accusing me, misusing me, and abusing me all over again. Then, when the chapter was turned, I saw another father. This father was warm, welcoming, forgiving, accepting, and loving with no conditions. This Father was

Jesus! God was showing the comparisons between my earthly father and my heavenly Father.

Immediately after this, God took me to a place within my vision where I was in a chapel-like place. I was kneeled with my arms folded and hands joined while Jesus stood in front of me. He had such a bright glow that saturated the entire room. As I cried my soul out to Jesus regarding my excruciating pain about my earthly father, Jesus stretched his arms to me. I then got up, walked to Jesus desperately sobbing and lamenting, and walked right into His outstretched arms. It was at this remarkable and unspeakable moment that Jesus picked me up in His arms, carried me to the pew, sat me in His lap, and rocked me back and forth! This was the most profound moment in my healing process and in my entire life! It was the most liberating feeling in the entire world and it was real in me!

> It was at this moment that God showed me that *He* was my daddy!
> Not just my father in heaven, but my daddy!
> He revealed to me that the relationship He has with His children is a personal one; if only we could comprehend the depth of it!
> In that moment, God was my daddy!

For twenty years, I had dreamed of my earthly father wiping my tears when I cried, holding me in his lap assuring me that I was special and worthy. In this moment, I received it all from Jesus (my Daddy)! God became everything that I was missing in a daddy. Everything! Jesus held me and rocked me and was patient with me. He assured me that He loved me in spite of. He assured me that it was okay and that He was here for me the way a daddy is supposed to be there. Can you say wow?

You see, God already knew that by me detaching myself from my earthly daddy as my source, I would gain deliverance and an unchangeable source within Him. What if I had never recognized and denounced my strongholds? What if I had never followed through with the process of casting down imaginations? What if I had never sought God to change my way of thinking to match His way of thinking? I would still be in chains today. However, I am a Diva unchained! God led me to call my daddy to talk to him exactly nine months after our last interaction.

For the first time ever, my daddy gave me a very sincere apology and said how he was in the wrong.

For the very first time, he did not blame his actions on drugs, but on his own foolishness and his own demons.

For the first time ever, my daddy did exactly what I wanted which was for him to apologize with no excuses.

For the first time in almost two years, I was able to talk to him without tears, without breaking, without falling to the floor, without my insides rattling, without anxiety attacks, and without flashbacks (related to PTSD) of my traumatic past.

In fact, when I went to my hometown one day, as we were leaving to head back home, I asked my husband to stop by my childhood house. I had always viewed this house as the most dreadful place to go in America. It was the one that my daddy did drugs in. The one that my daddy got drunk in. The one that my daddy abused my mother in. The one that my brother almost killed himself in. The one that my daddy molested me in.

As I went in, I looked throughout the house and remembered everything. Vividly.

But all of a sudden, the house was no longer a threat to me as it had been all those years.

I realized that I no longer associated the house with pain. I now associated the house as part of the process to reaching my purpose and destiny. To my delight, I smiled.

I smiled because this was where Satan planned for my purpose to die.

But on the flip side, this is where God used Satan's plan to birth my purpose! I smiled because I was no longer stuck in this house within my mind. Because I had broken the chains of the strongholds, I now held the power over the entire house and every past scene!

"This is where I'm from. This is not who I am. This is no longer my house or my life. This is where Satan planned for me to die. This is where Satan planned for my life to be destroyed. But I won. Satan, you and the ghosts of this house have lost your power over me. I won! I don't regret this house. I won! God and I conquered you Satan. Look at me now! So thank you 123 North Sever Street. Thank you. Bye. And this time, it's really Goodbye."

I literally left smiling.

This is what God will do for you once you seek Him to reveal your strongholds that Satan has placed in your mind; once you denounce all strongholds, fight daily using prayer and God's word, and bring all thoughts to obey the thoughts of Christ. Really, you've already won, but you must take the steps to activate that victory.

Yes, the process is often painful, but the reward is fruitful and abundant! Sometimes, we feel regret and a sense of loss. We feel like our time was wasted going through our trials. We feel like we lost so much and that we could have accomplished so much in our lives if we had not experienced such hostile trials. However, the truth is that God makes up for all losses.

There is no way to describe it and you cannot even fathom

how He will do it. I assure you that God has a way of making up for everything that you feel you lost or missed out on. God said that He will "Restore the years to you that the locust, cankerworm, and caterpillar have eaten" (Joel 2:25).

In other words, God is saying He is going to repay you for everything that you have lost. Everything that the enemy has stolen (joy, peace, finances, stability, accomplishments, etc.) shall be returned unto you. For every single year that was affected by life's lemons and strongholds, God will restore unto you Ms. Diva! This is a promise.

God said even the things you didn't even know that were yours before will be restored unto you! **The process is what brings forth the promises.** You must endure the process, God's way!

After it's all said and done, the devil wants us to think that we've lost those things. However, God stores up our blessings. He has them in His hands waiting to release them unto you; waiting on you to seek Him to tear down these strongholds. He stores your blessings, and when you have successfully completed the process His way, the blessings are released as an overflow unto you! I'm a witness!

I have received my overflow and I want you to receive yours!

God wants you to get to the point to where you understand that everything that you are enduring was already conquered on the cross by Jesus. It has been done in the heavenly realms for you. However, you (only you) must take action in the earth in order for it to occur. "Whatsoever ye shall bind on earth shall be bound in heaven: and whatsoever ye shall loose on earth shall be loosed in heaven" (Matthew 18:18).

To bind means to imprison...

Chain it up...

Or to forbid it from happening.

To loose means to release; to unchain. What are you binding with the words that you speak? What are you loosing with the words that you speak? You have the power to bind up every stronghold that has kept you in chains! You have the power to loose every blessing that belongs to you! God says once you use your power to do this on the earth, it shall be done in the heavens and shall manifest in the earth.

Whatever it may be, you've been in chains too long!

It's time for *you* to chain up your strongholds, struggles, adversaries; and free your peace, joy, and blessings.

Speak the command!

Declare the scripture (Matthew 18:18).

And break the strongholds!

I spoke the commands with power. I commanded every single unholy attachment to be bound up. I bound up the spirit of depression, the spirit of deceit and ignorance that tried to keep me from knowing my purpose, and the spirit of fear. I bound the spirit of PTSD because I realized that even that was the result of a spiritual stronghold that was out to destroy my destiny. I bound up the unholy soul tie with my daddy; the one that convinced me that my purpose was attached to him and not to God. I bound up the strongholds as a result of the sexual abuse and every health problem that came to attack my body and mind.

I loosed peace, joy, favor, wholeness in my body, thoughts and a mind like Christ, activation of my purpose and destiny, assurance that my purpose is attached to my relationship with God and not man, a healing for the little girl in me, deliverance for me, and every blessing of God that rightfully belongs to me in Jesus' name.

As a result of breaking the strongholds off of my life, I have freedom in my life like I've never felt before. I have a peace and joy about myself and life that I didn't even know was possible! God restored my self-worth, peace, and gave me back my voice! It's one thing to be financially prosperous as I am, but it's a whole new blessing to be emotionally and spiritually prosperous. My emotions are not all over the place anymore. I don't fall down at the sound of my daddy's name anymore. My nerves are much better. My mind is stable. I don't fear people shooting through my house anymore. I don't run every time I hear my kids make a sound with the fear that something tragic has happened. I don't fear my daddy abusing me anymore. I smile from within now instead of smiling to hide my pain.

I learned to love myself again. Moreover, I see myself the way God sees me! I regained my courage and confidence. I now *know* that I am free and I walk in that freedom!

I feel safe at home with my husband, the man who was there by my side the entire process. I realize that this new great home and this phenomenal family that I have now is my life, not my childhood home. Moreover Ms. Diva, I realize that I have overcome! I have not only left my past behind physically, but I have put it out of my mind and have guarded my heart from it.

Even on my hard days, I know how to go to God when I'm having a fatherless moment. I know how to get into a safe place to allow God to give me every sense of warmth, protection, and validation that I need. And it feels good! I know how to refrain from going into depression, hopelessness, and helplessness.

I am free from anxiety attacks! Not only did I turn all my lemons into lemonade and am abundantly eating of the good of the land, but I also tore down the enemy's camp and took back everything that he had stolen from me! It belonged to me and I took it! My prayer is that you too, will go into the enemy's camp, tear down his walls, and take back what belongs to you! The battles in your life are spiritual and the only way to fight the enemy is with spiritual weapons. Use your Bible and prayer to break the chains against your life. God and His angels are cheering for you Ms. Diva! I declare that you are no longer enchained. You are a DIVA Unchained!

Do not give Satan the satisfaction by staying a victim! Rely on God's power to turn you into a victor. Your lemons are not the end of your destiny! Through God, you have the power to break every chain of stronghold against your life. As I always say...*You can be free. You can be healed. You can be whole!*

9

The Gifted Cry

❦

Have you ever felt that a person cannot give you advice or help you with anything unless they've been through what you've been through? Oftentimes, a person can reach another person more effectively if they have experienced a similar trial. The trials that you experience can be used to tremendously help someone one day because you have firsthand experience. You may be going through a hard trial in your life as you read this book. If you are not, you may have gone through a very rough time previously. Maybe your time has not come just yet, but God knows it is on the way. Either way, this virtue of *Inspiration* will benefit you and open up your eyes to a whole new way of looking at your trials. If I had known years ago what I know now, I would not have been so depressed during my trials. I'm honored that God has equipped me to inform you of these things so that you can make better decisions. God says that whatever trial you are experiencing, it won't always be like this. "For our present troubles are small and won't last very long. Yet, they produce for us a glory that vastly outweighs them and will last forever" (II Corinthians 4:17 NLT). God said your trials are temporary. Even though it seems long while you are going through, hold on, because you will be rewarded for your faithfulness. You must endure, stay prayerful, and faithful.

My Diva sister, do not prolong your trial by staying depressed like I used to do. Do not prolong your trial by continuing to be angry, regretful, or sad. God looks at your response to situations. You must practice responding to your trials with faith and watch God move on your behalf. God operates off of faith; not fear, anger, depression, or regrets. Don't throw yourself a pity party for the devil to feed on.

Why Must We Suffer?

Remember that the situation or trial that you are experiencing is meant to be used to edify someone else in the future. God allows certain things to happen for a reason. It's so that He can get the glory out of it. An example can be found in the book of John with the blind man where we learn that *not all* suffering is the result of sin.

"Neither this man nor his parents sinned…but this happened so that the works of God might be displayed in him" (John 9:3 NIV).

Yes, many times we suffer because of sin. God must punish sin because He is holy.

However, sometimes, a person's suffering is *not* due to sin. Sometimes, the suffering is because God wants to get the glory out of us.

He wants to show that He alone is the only one able to work miracles and turn situations around. Jesus restored the blind man's sight which was something that only He could do. Like the blind man, some of your trials are so that God may show His mercy, mature you, elevate you, or use you as a vessel to edify others. God sees every tear that you cry. He knows and cares about every pain that you endure. He allows you to endure trials so that you can grow and become an inspiration to others.

According to Webster dictionary, to inspire means *to influence or to guide someone in a divine or supernatural way.* Anytime you see the word divine, it means heavenly or Godly. So, when you inspire someone, you guide them and influence them in a Godly way.

This is God's desire: to take our trials, pains, disgusts, guilt, and disappointments and use them to inspire someone to grow in their walk with God. Listen, God never promised you that you won't have trials. He said, "...Have peace in me. Here on earth, you will have many trials and sorrows, but take heart, because I have overcome the world" (John

> *God allows your trials; your trials cause your tears; and your tears activate your anointing.*

16:33 NLT). In other words, you must expect to be afflicted and have trials. Nevertheless, there is good news! Jesus has already conquered your trials on the cross. We are not supposed to be surprised at our trials (1 Peter 4:12-13). We should not think it's strange that we experience such fiery trials because the trials are meant to test our responses and strengthen our faith. Contrary to what we believe, we are supposed to rejoice in our sufferings. By rejoicing in our trials, we actually participate in the suffering of Jesus when he was crucified. When we look to Jesus during our suffering, we are drawn closer to Jesus on the cross where He endured betrayal, discouragement, neglect, abandonment, heartbreak, and excruciating pain—to say the least. Our suffering is designed to draw ourselves and others closer to Jesus.

Your Tears Activate Your Anointing

There is an anointing activated by your cry when your cry is unto the Lord. Everyone cries at some point. Some people cry to loved ones and some people choose to cry alone. However, when your cry is from the trials that God has allowed in your life, and you take those issues to God and cry unto Him, your tears bring forth the anointing from within you. "Now he who establishes us…with Christ, and anointed us, is God; who also sealed us, and gave us the down payment of the Spirit in our hearts" (II Corinthians 1:21-22 WEB). We receive God's spirit within us the minute we become saved. Furthermore, God breathed life into us. Therefore, if His breath lives within us, God's spirit comes as part of the package.

The crying out from your trial is what helps to activate the anointing. Why is this so? It is because your trials were already stamped and approved by God. The scripture above tells us that God sealed us and gave us the Spirit as a down payment. God expects you to give back what He has stored within you. He has stored the anointing. He has allowed that trial so that it will cause you to cry unto Him. In crying unto God, He activates that anointing within you and causes you to grow and inspire.

The Book of Luke Chapter Seven gives the story of a sinful woman with an alabaster box of ointment. The Bible says she was a woman of many sins. She was in need of salvation and the forgiveness of her sins. She knew that there was only one way to get her blessing. Therefore, when she saw Jesus, she kissed His feet and washed His feet with her tears. She then anointed His feet with oil. Jesus said to the woman, "Your faith has made you whole." He healed her and forgave her because she had the appropriate response; faith and submission to Jesus.

Remember this: God allows your trials, your trials cause your tears, and your tears activate your anointing. If you never endure a trial, you will never cry those types of tears, which means your anointing remains bottled up. The anointing is what empowers you to inspire others. Allow God to take those trials and turn them into triumphs.

Your anointing grows out of your pain, heartaches, disappointments, etc. I do not know exactly what trial this woman was experiencing, but we know that she was in deep sin and was scarred by it. This woman teaches us two things.

Number one, we should surrender to God first through prayer in the midst of our adversities. *Secondly*, we are to bless Him even in the midst of our afflictions. In the midst of her trials and pain, the woman with the alabaster box cried unto Jesus for her healing which showed that she acknowledged Him as being the only one able to miraculously bless her. She was not selfish in her request. She blessed Jesus by anointing His feet.

Too often, we take our pain to friends, family, and social networks before ever surrendering in prayer to Jesus. We tend to expect things from God without ever blessing Him. Your pain, hurt, disappointments, heartache, guilt, or shame is all meant to produce the anointing of God so that you will be able to take it, be empowered by it, and inspire someone else. It's okay to go to others sometimes and talk about your problems. It's okay to cry to others sometimes if it's someone that can lend an open ear, give you great advice, or pray with you. A loved one who knows the Lord, a pastor, a Christian counselor, or psychologist are all examples of people you can go to with your tears.

However, in the midst of your crying, make sure you cry out *unto Jesus, our Lord.* When you cry, God's intention is for you to take the tears to Him in the same manner that the woman with the alabaster box took her tears to Jesus. When the lady cried, she was on her knees at Jesus' feet. Her gift came when she kneeled at Jesus' feet and cried out from her pain. Pray about everything! *When you cry, kneel at Jesus' feet and allow your anointed tears to fall at His feet.* This is where your breakthrough will come. This is where your blessings will come. Whatever the situation is that has you bound, there is an anointing inside of you waiting to be used by God. So it's okay to cry, my Diva sister. Just make sure you have the right attitude towards your trial. The key is remembering this: God's purpose within your pain is to use those tears to activate your anointing.

Remember that it won't always be like this! It is even medically beneficial for you to cry through any trials that you may experience because it helps to relieve stress.

Andrea Buchanan, author of the *Women's Health* article *Go with the Flow,* informs us that when we are stressed, our bodies get filled with stress hormones such as cortisol and other toxins. [1] Therefore, crying is actually our body's way of removing stress hormones and toxic chemicals from our bodies. [1] This proves that crying heals us physically, but crying also heals us spiritually. Just as tears eject toxic chemicals from your physical body, God wants to (spiritually) remove the toxic chemicals of anger, bitterness, depression, hurt, jealousy, and/or defeat. He wants to remove all these toxic chemicals so that He can activate His anointing within you.

Bear Your Cross

Eventually, throughout this deliverance process, you may be required to forgive others, let go of some things such as resentment, regret, grudges, or sinful habits. I had to forgive my father in order to obtain more of what God had for me. God literally stripped me down before He built me back up! God took me off my job, told me to leave work, find a therapist, and focus on my soul. I was standing outside leaning against my car when I asked God why did I have to experience such dreadful things with my daddy. I basically asked God why I had to lose my daddy: the relationship I craved and felt I needed so badly. I asked why I had to lose the man who I had held on to for almost two decades.

My lamentation to God:

"God, I've been through some of the hardest battles there were to experience. God, I've endured some of the toughest pain there could be and I still stayed faithful to you. But God, this right here—this is the one thing that I can't seem to let go. That's my daddy God! Why my daddy God? Why did the incest have to happen? Why my daddy, whom I need so much? Why did you allow him to leave me, then abuse me? God, I can take anything else. But not this Lord! Why?"

That's when God replied very firmly,
"Your daddy was your sacrifice!"

I paused for a very long time because that cut me like a sword, but it also provided some clarity and relief.

I could do nothing but reverence God and accept His position on this matter.

My sacrifice?

Wow!

Immediately, God provided clarification within my spirit about what He meant. God revealed to me that we all have a cross to bear. Our own sacrifices. Jesus was God's sacrifice. Jesus' life was His sacrifice. Abraham leaving his family and his home behind was his sacrifice. Job's loss of his children and possessions was his sacrifice. And so on.

Jesus tells us that we must pick up our cross and follow Him (Matthew 16:24). You see, we all have a cross to bear. Every single soul on this earth must bear trials in some way.

You must understand that my daddy was my world. Out of every child, he and I had the closest bond. To lose him (to drugs

God's purpose within your pain is to use those tears to activate your anointing.

and to the system) at such a young age was absolutely devastating! He meant everything to me! At that time (age 7 and younger), all I knew from him was love. I didn't see anything else. The sexual abuse didn't occur until I was a teenager, **and it ripped me into shreds,** because like most little girls, I saw my daddy as my first love.

And now, the *thought* of losing him broke me!

That's why God said my daddy was my sacrifice. Losing my daddy like I did through the series of tumultuous events and then, being directed to lose my relationship with him was indeed my sacrifice and a mighty cross to bear! It hurt severely to hear and have to accept that from God. God was telling me that it was something that He was going to heal me from, but it's also something that I would have to carry with me as I follow Him.

I figured maybe in another world, I can be daddy's little girl.

Maybe he can dance *innocently* with me, teach me everything he knows about the Bible, hold me *innocently,* and wipe my tears when I need him.

Maybe in another world…but for now, it's my cross to bear for the kingdom of God!

Just like Jesus himself picked up His own cross (*that was of no sin that He did*), and prevailed to His destiny, you and I must pick up our own cross and prevail to our destiny—with faith that God will provide the grace and strength.

What is that one major thing that you just can't seem to let go? Can't seem to get over? Can't seem to understand why? The one thing you would give everything to go back in time and reverse? That thing may just be your personal sacrifice to God. That one thing may just be your cross that you must learn to pick up and follow Jesus.

Yes, you must still cast down any and all strongholds attached to the event or trial. However, just like Jesus knew that the cross was inevitable and was a part of His destiny, you must know too that your cross is inevitable and is a part of your destiny. It's time for you to pick it up, give it to God, and follow Jesus in order to fulfill your life purpose and reach your destiny.

Tears & Gifts

The key is remembering that your cry is gifted. Your cry will bring about your blessings just as the woman's tears on Jesus' feet brought along her blessing. Whether you are a teenager or an adult, it is equally important for you to pray. Don't choose to suffer through your problems without reaping the blessings that God has for you. "Do not worry about anything; instead, pray about everything. Tell God what you need, and thank Him for all He has done" (Philippians 4:6 NLT).

The Holy Spirit gives many different spiritual gifts.

God has given spiritual gifts to all Christians. "Now there are different kinds of spiritual gifts, but the same Spirit...God works in different ways, but it is the same God who does the work in all of us. A Spiritual gift is given to each of us so we can help each other" (I Corinthians 12:4-7 NLT). The difference between spiritual gifts and talents is the manner in which it is used. Spiritual gifts are given by the Holy Spirit and are used to uplift God's people or to add to the body of Christ in some way. Sometimes, people use their Spiritual gifts for the wrong thing. Some people stick it in a bottle and never use it. However, all Spiritual gifts are supposed to be used to glorify God and edify ourselves and His people.

Believe it or not, God allows things to happen to you to take you to another level. He wants to help you grow in your gift. **Whatever it is that you've been going through that has led you to the cry is probably the same area God wants to use you in!**

Most people that you see in ministries that are prospering have experienced the things they are now helping others in. The drug and alcohol counselor may have been an addict before or may have been a victim as a child whose parent was an addict.

The woman that helps rape victims was probably a previous victim of rape. That woman that can sing a worship song such as "For Every Mountain" with so much anointing that people fall to the floor is probably a woman that God has brought out of many pitfalls.

My mother always tells me, "Salvation is free, but the anointing is expensive!" Those people paid a price for their gifts. They experienced some tough situations, endured them, and conquered them through the blood of Jesus.

That's why I always tell others, *"Don't envy my overflow because you don't know the cost of my oil." What I went through would've killed other people! The anointing on my life is expensive!* There's a song by Marvin Sapp called "Place of Worship". [2] In the song, he sings, "Every tear you cried is water for the garden of your victory." He tells us that victory comes through your adversity; your trials. He then says, "Look into your pain and find your praise." This is what you have to do Ms. Diva. Even though it's okay for you to cry, it is never okay for you to stay in a low place. You must find your praise even in your low place.

Just like the rain waters the garden to grow the plants and flowers, every single tear that you cry helps to water the garden of your victory and your spiritual gifts. **Your cry gives birth to your Spiritual Gift.** So go ahead and cry. Let God mold you, grow you, and perfect the anointing and the spiritual gift that is within you. Let your trials inspire you. Don't wait until you're fifty years old to use your Spiritual gifts and reap the blessings that God has for you.

I was the person that didn't know my Spiritual gifts for a while. Before God showed me, I would always say, "I don't have talents. I don't have gifts. I don't know how to do much!" But girl, was I mistaken! I've never been more wrong! If you are someone that feels you have no gifts like I did, pray and ask God to make you aware of the Spiritual gifts He has given you. When you pray for it, be sure to *look* for it!

Learn to take what the devil is doing and use it on him. In order to find out the Spiritual gifts, read I Corinthians 12. When you find out your individual gifts, use those gifts to cry out to

God and to glorify God during your trials. There are things to do to help edify you as you go through a trial. If you know how to sing, cry out through songs. If you have a gift of dance, cry out through dance. If you love to write poetry, cry out through poetry. If you have a gift of speaking, cry out and glorify God in presenting speeches to others. Whether it's playing instruments, drawing, painting, or designing jewelry, find a way to use that gift to cry out and glorify God. No matter whom you are or what you have experienced, you have been given some kind of gift. Whatever the case may be, it is never healthy to suppress your pain. You must cry out in some way.

There is a gift within your cry!

10

Dare to Inspire

❧

Once God reveals your spiritual gift and you are inspired, God expects you to inspire others with your gift. As I have previously stated, God anoints you within the trial if you respond the right way. 1 Thessalonians 5:11 says, "Therefore encourage one another and build each other up" (NIV). Once God activates that Spiritual Gift within you, you can then inspire others! How do you inspire others? Where do you start? First, you pray to God and ask that He shows you what's in His will for you to do. You then seek within yourself and look into your heart. It will more than likely go along with the spiritual gift that God has for you. It's usually tied to your passions that won't seem to disappear. I know a woman that inspires others through poetry. She absolutely loves to write and recite poems. Her words minister so strongly to others. This is one of her gifts. She says, "All I ever wanted to do was poetry!" Think about your gift that we spoke about in the "Gifted Cry" chapter. Your inspirational calling will more than likely be tied to your gift and passion that's already in you. Is your gift singing? Writing Speeches? Organizing Events? Designing? Playing Instruments? Styling Hair? Dancing? Get involved in your church or an organization with whatever your gift is.

God expects you to work.

The Bible says, "I must work the works of him that sent me while it's day. The night cometh, when no man can work" (John 9:4). Don't miss out on the opportunity to work where God is working. Make the best out of the little time that we are on this Earth. We are to work *where* He says work and *when* He says to work. It's on God's timing, not ours. You don't have time to waste. The Lord said if you keep quiet and do not serve Him, He will have the stones to cry out in your place (Luke 19:40). Don't let rocks cry out for you! Use the gift God gave you to inspire others! God has already empowered you to do it. You just have to activate the power that's within you.

Custom-Made Battles Equal Custom-Made Inspirations

Once I understood the power that I had to help others based on the trials I experienced, I felt a world of difference! I felt my importance in life. I thought, "God, you allowed me to go through all this so that I could help bring souls to you and help save those who are on the verge of giving up on life. God, you made me to be a light to those in darkness." I knew I was definitely special to God! I remember talking to a young lady who tried to kill herself. She was abused as a teenager and was in her early twenties. She felt like she was nothing; of no importance to the world. That's the trick of the enemy to make us feel that way. When I began to tell her my story about how God brought me out of abuse, a house of drug addiction, and my own suicidal attempts, she was astounded. When God brings you out, He makes all things new! No one can tell what

I've been through just by looking at me. A lot of people think that I come from such a perfect life. I love telling my story now because people look at the grace and favor over my life and become stunned when they find out the things I've been through. They are able to see God's power working in and through me.

I love telling my story because my story changes lives!

My story helps to save lives!

My story ministers to others!

My story inspires and empowers others!

There were times when I just *knew* that the things I was going through were going to kill me. I was sure it would all take me out or cause me to be in a mental institution. However, my Diva sister, what we go through is not meant to kill us. It's meant to make us stronger in the Lord.

Your story can inspire others as well! A lot of people respond wrongly to situations and never receive what God wants them to receive. When you go through situations, you must pray and ask God what He wants you to learn or do based on the trials that you experience. Sometimes it's for your own personal and spiritual growth.

Sometimes, it's for you to inspire others.

Remember that it won't always be like this!

The Bible says that the trials that we go through are only for a moment, but it works in our favor far greater than the actual pain of the trial (II Corinthians 4:17).

For five years, I oversaw a mentoring ministry in which I implemented many functions and practices to help young ladies achieve their goals, grow in their relationships with God, learn to deal with their afflictions, and more. God led me to begin an annual Girls program within a high school I taught at. After a few prosperous years, God enlarged my territory and expanded my program into the communities. The program that

I founded is a registered product of my nonprofit organization and is a very rewarding experience for the participants as well as myself. In addition to my Life Coach & Counseling Practice, I oversee several other projects and activities for women and girls that truly change their lives. I am able to do all of this because I was inspired to *inspire* others. It is because of the trials and hardships that I experienced that allow me to efficiently empower those girls through the grace of God. If I had not experienced what I did, I would not be able to provide these at-risk girls with prevention and intervention services. God didn't want me to wallow in my adversities; He wanted me to use my adversities to inspire others! Suicide is the third most common cause of death in children from ages 10 to 19 and it is proven that girls attempt suicide more often than boys.[1]

None of this was missed by God. Before I was even born, God already knew the rapidly increasing rate of suicide and depression that would occur among girls as well as women. He ordained me to be one of the many ones to intervene and interrupt Satan's plan among young girls and women. My trials were designed just for me in order to equip me to do this work. Not only were my trials custom-made, but my gifts were also custom-made. You are no different! Your battles were stamped with God's approval to shape your destiny just as your gift was tailored to fit your inspirational calling.

Your Brokenness is Someone Else's Healing

To know that what I experienced was in order that I may impact the lives of women and girls; to help guide them to the destiny God has designed for them; and to show them a new way of seeing life, makes me proud that I survived what I did. It makes me thankful to God that I actually went through the tough times. I would never want to experience those turbulent trials again; nevertheless, I'm thankful to have endured and conquered! I didn't always have that kind of attitude. I had to realize that when we are experiencing trials, it doesn't seem like it will ever get better, but the Bible tells us differently. No trial seems pleasant during the times we experience it and even though it seems like it is unbearable at the time, it is always for our profit (see Hebrews 12:11). I remember asking the Lord, "How come all these horrible things always happen to me?" God's response was, "**Understand that you are a threat to the enemy.**" At that moment, I realized that the bigger the threat, the bigger the attacks.

I understood that I had a purpose in life and a reason to keep going. I acknowledged the great calling that I had on my life and the amount of lives God was going to change through me. You too, have been called to make a difference in the lives of others. This could mean volunteering at an agency or shelter, making jewelry with inspirational messages, writing blogs and poetry for others, or whatever your heart sees fit. No spiritual gift is small. As my husband Coral says, "Your brokenness is tied to someone else's healing". If it seems like you never get a break, remember it's because you are a threat to Satan's Kingdom! Run on to see what the end is going to be. Endure your trials and inspire others like you were called to do. God is calling you Ms. Diva. So, be inspired to inspire others!

VIRTUE THREE

The 'V' In DIVAS

VISION

"A vivid mental image [that combines your dreams and God's plans for you]. One that you can picture before it happens. Something that you see or dream especially as part of a religious or supernatural experience."

Key Bible Scripture

"Write the vision and make it plain upon the tables..."

~Habakkuk 2:2

11

The Face of Confidence

و∽

N ow that you are inspired, it's time to focus on your vision and God's vision for your life. Your vision could be your dreams, goals, or desires for your life. Before you can grasp the virtue of *vision,* you must have confidence. This chapter will focus on gaining and strengthening confidence.What flaws do you think you have? What do you not like about yourself? Take a minute to think about them and list your top three flaws or personal dislikes below.

_____

_____

_____

We will get to your list a little later. For now, let's look closely at the definition of confidence. Webster defines confidence as "a state of mind or manner marked by coolness and freedom from uncertainty, shyness, or embarrassment; not worrying about failure or disapproval of others." Confidence is when you embrace what you (or others) see as flaws. Confidence is being free from a feeling of embarrassment. It is being certain about yourself and your strengths. Confidence does not mean being conceited or thinking that you are better than others. *Confidence means recognizing your flaws, but capitalizing your strengths.* In other words, you learn to accept what you and others see as imperfections and find a way to be comfortable with them or use them to your advantage. Confidence is when you stop giving all the power to your flaws and begin to benefit from your strengths. You focus on your strengths and build on them. Confidence is when you learn to gain energy from your strengths instead of losing energy from your flaws.

Let's talk more of what confidence looks like in what I call "The Face of Confidence". In order to visualize this, think of a simple smiley face.

THE FACE OF CONFIDENCE

The Forehead: *Hold your head up high.* A person with confidence holds their head up high. They never allow anyone or anything to make them walk with their head down. You may have a big nose. So what! Hold your head up high! You are just as important as the person with the smaller nose. You deserve to walk with your head held high!

The Eyes: *See beyond your flaws.* This is one of the hardest things for a person with low confidence to do. Contradictorily, it's also one of the most important things for a person to do. Seeing beyond your flaws means accepting you for who you are. More importantly, it means being able to see the greatness in you that God sees in you; focusing more on your strengths and your beauty than on your weaknesses and flaws. Everything that God made was good; and yes my Diva sister, that includes *you*! It means to stop enlarging your weaknesses and start enlarging your strengths. How long will you focus on your flaws?

How long will you give weight to your weaknesses?

How long will you allow your flaws to shut you up, sit you down, and belittle you?

It's so much more beyond your flaws. *Flaws make you unique, not small.* Flaws are a small piece of you, not all of you. **Flaws are the minority; you (and every other positive trait that makes you) are the majority.** There's so much more to enjoy and to love about yourself. But you must see it! A person with low self-confidence sees a mole when others merely see a dot. No matter what your flaws may be, you must be able to see your bigger attributes that make you wonderful in God's eyesight. You must be able to see beyond your flaws and see all that God has placed in you to excel in every area of your life.

The Nose: *Blow off the Criticism of others.* We are human and we all have to blow our nose sometimes to remove foreign particles that clog our nose and sinuses. With "The Face of Confidence", the nose is used to blow off the criticism of others. People with confidence smell the criticism of others, but don't let it determine their actions. They still do what's best for them regardless of what others think. If people say you cannot play volleyball well, but it's something you love to do, confidence says you will do it anyway despite what others say or think. You are not trying to please them! You are trying to fulfill your desires of playing a sport. Remember, confidence does not mean you are the *best* at everything. It means you are free from being embarrassed about it.

The Mouth: *Accept Compliments*. The normal purpose of the mouth is to speak, but with the "The Face of Confidence", its purpose is to accept compliments that people give you. Being confident means you are capable of accepting compliments. In the past, I had the hardest time accepting compliments. The reason was that I had such low confidence that I was not able to believe the compliments. Once a person is able to accept compliments, it shows that she has *recognized her flaws, but has set her focus on her strengths.*

Where Does it Come from?

A lack of confidence usually comes from not feeling worthy of praise, feeling unloved, feeling un-wanted, or feeling un-important. Low confidence can also come from not recognizing who God says you are. Additionally, low confidence can come from childhood experiences such as **not** receiving a lot of compliments as a child and/or receiving a lot of criticism from people who you expect to show love. For example, if a mother or father calls you out of your name and belittles you as a child, this can cause you to feel low, which causes a lack of confidence. Similarly, if a mom or dad never tells you how beautiful you are or how talented you are, this can also create low confidence.

Much of my low confidence came from my dad. It took me over a decade to realize this. I don't want you to wait that long to tackle your underlying issues.

My dad called me every kind of bitch and motherfucker in the book. He randomly got mad and started calling me names like I was someone on the street. I couldn't understand that. I thought to myself, "But I'm his daughter." The more he called me those names, the more I started to feel low about myself. I didn't realize it then, but when I finally decided to surrender all my pain to God, He showed me that I had begun to internalize it as a child.

Every bitch that I was called; every time my daddy told me I was nothing, some sub-conscious part of me began to believe it. I thought for so long that I was nothing. Although my daddy told me I was beautiful and important when I was a little girl, it stopped at the age of seven when he went to prison several states away. When he returned after six years, I do not think I ever heard my daddy call me beautiful again until I was an adult. He no longer told me I deserved nice things. He no longer told me I was going to be someone great in life or that I was important.

The only thing that he continued to tell me was that I was smart. And I tell you no lies: this is the only positive thing that I continued to believe about myself. I had confidence that I was smart so I continued to excel in school.

Do you see how much of an impact loved ones can have on your confidence? **The absence of compliments can be just as detrimental to your confidence as the presence of criticisms.** It may not be your mother or father that contributed to your low confidence. It could be a boyfriend, a sister, a brother or a very close friend. However, it is crucial that you learn to identify the things that cause your low self-confidence and find a method to overcome them.

How Do You Strengthen Confidence?

To help me with my low confidence areas, God gave me an acronym. I want to share my strategy with you to help you improve your confidence. It has helped my very own daughter and hundreds of girls within my nonprofit organization. All you have to do is picture the word *PAT*. In order to improve your confidence, you must P.A.T. yourself on the back every now and again. When you hear yourself speaking criticism toward yourself, reverse the criticism into a compliment and P.A.T. yourself on the back.

The meaning of the acronym P.A.T. is listed below.

Pat yourself on the back every now and again.

*P*ick positive thoughts.
*A*ct on approval from God and not from Men.
*T*rust who God says you are!

Pick Positive Thoughts

The very moment that you begin to think about your low confidence areas or the negative things others say about you, the first thing you need to do is pick positive thoughts.

Philippians 4:8 says, "*Whatsoever things are true, whatsoever things are honest, whatsoever things are just, whatsoever things are pure, whatsoever things are lovely, whatsoever things are of good report; if there be any virtue, and if there be any praise, think on these things.*"

In other words, take the bad things and find the good things within them. The good things, the true things, the pure things, and the lovely things are what you should focus on. The first step is to *pick positive thoughts!*

Act on Approval from God, Not Men

People with low self-confidence usually do things based on what others think. Remember the second half of the definition of confidence is "not worrying about failure or disapproval from others." All your life, someone, somewhere is going to criticize you or have something negative to say about you. However, you must learn to act on approval from God and not from men.

Our competence comes from God. When we focus on what God approves, we can become more at peace with ourselves. You can be assured that if God has placed His stamp of approval on something, then no one else's approval matters. When I felt God was leading me to apply for a position as Graduation Coach at a high school, I thought to myself, "How in the world am I going to help increase the graduation rate and decrease the rate of the amount of kids dropping out of high school? I can't do this."

꽃

Confidence means recognizing your flaws, but capitalizing your strengths.

I thought about all of my low confidence areas regarding my short height and my perceived squeaky voice and I told God and myself, "No one is going to listen to me. I'm nobody." Then, I picked a positive thought (the P in P.A.T) saying, "I may be just the person those kids need!" I chose to act on the fact that God had approved me for that position. That was all that mattered! As a result, I got into that position and made a remarkable difference in the lives of so many of those students. God truly used me to help some students come back to school after deciding to drop out of high school. Because of my counsel, many students who were skipping school started going to class. You see, the approval from people don't matter. What God says is what matters! The Bible tells us, "Stop regarding man, whose breath of life is in his nostrils; For why should he be esteemed" (Isaiah 2:22 NASB)? We should not place so much value on the opinions and criticisms of people. Their lives are nothing but breath. Our lives are just vapors. This is why you should **only** act from the approval of God—the one who breathed the life into the nostrils of man. If those people whom you seek approval from were to stop breathing, what would you do at that point? The source that you depend on to give you approval should be an *eternal* source which is God alone.

Trust Who God Says You Are

Who are you? In addition to picking positive thoughts and acting on approval from God, you must also trust who God say you are. You find out who God says you are through prayer, reading God's word, and even hearing Him directly. Sometimes, it can come by way of people speaking into your life: They randomly say *positive* things about you and your life. The same thing is often repeated by different people as confirmation. What have people said about you that you rejected? It could have been God speaking! There have been many times in the past that I rejected when God spoke through people about me. I rejected it all because of my low confidence areas. I saw myself as this useless person that was forgotten about by God and could not do anything helpful. I thought my life was a waste. This is why I rejected it. I thought to myself, "There is no way those things are true of me." People spoke things into my life that I did not even realize were from God.

They said things like: "Girl, you are going somewhere great in life!" "You are an awesome speaker." "You are so anointed!"

When they said these things, I would verbally reject them. I would respond, "Unh unh, but I stumbled over some words when I spoke."

"Anointed? I don't know about that!"

The Bible says that life and death are in the power of the tongue (Proverbs 18:21).

You have to speak life, not death. When someone speaks positive things in your life, try the spirit by the spirit within you and see if it's of God. Then, make a conscientious decision to speak life. Do not reject the positive things that people speak into your life. Many times, its God letting you know how important you are to Him. He shows it to other people and they speak it to you. Don't be too busy focusing on your low confidence areas that you miss when God is trying to let you know who you are to Him! If you grasp the *P* in *PAT,* you will have already begun focusing on picking positive thoughts. This will allow you to receive the *T* and trust who God says you are.

Once I stopped rejecting who God says I am, I was able to see His vision for my life. I was able to see those things that had been spoken begin to manifest in my life. You see, God tells you who you are and what you will be even before you can see it. God doesn't see you like you are now; He sees you like you will be when you fully walk in His will. However, you must be the one to make the decision to trust who God says you are and walk in it!

Embrace what you see as flaws. We are not supposed to be perfect! **We get our strength from God because we have weaknesses. We get our approval from God because we have uncertainties. We get our confidence from God because we have flaws!** But even in all of our flaws, uncertainties, and weaknesses, we must remember that we were *fearfully* and *wonderfully* made! That's enough to be bold and confident.

~

90% of all women want to change at least one aspect of their physical appearance. [1]

The Corner of Confidence

When God began to restore my confidence, He directed me to write down my positive attributes and gifts. I sat down, and in a matter of minutes, I had about thirty sticky notes of amazing attributes about myself. I then stuck all the sticky notes in what I called my "Corner of Confidence". It was a corner of my bathroom mirror where I lined up all my sticky notes so that every single morning, I would be greeted with those very true, positive, traits about myself. My sticky notes consisted of words and phrases such as:

> *Eloquent speaker, innovator, well educated, author, life coach, odd-beater, worthy, soldier, a woman of influence, unique, delivered, my life is meaningful, God is my daddy, trailblazer, counselor to many, go-getter, proverbs 31 wife, role model to women, extraordinary mother, visionary, beautiful, fearfully and wonderfully made.*

I didn't list one single flaw or failure-only positive characteristics and successes.

This way, I wouldn't be able to focus on the flaws or low confidence areas.

Every day, the amazing traits of mine became magnified and I began to see myself as God saw me. Each morning, I was greeted with a new way of seeing myself. As I looked at myself in the mirror each morning, more and more, I gained a new face of confidence. With each new day, these awesome attributes of mine began to overpower my failures and flaws that once led to my low confidence. I never denied my flaws or failures, but my corner of confidence wowed me so much that the flaws and failures just really didn't matter at all anymore! I finally knew who I was. And who I am—is *great*! And so are you Ms. Diva!

At the beginning of this chapter, I asked you to write down three things that you felt were your low confidence areas. Choose at least **one** of your low confidence areas and apply the *P.A.T.* method to help you overcome those areas. Recite your *P.A.T* strategy on a regular basis or whenever you are challenged in your level of confidence.

Choose 1 Low Confidence Area

_____

Increase Your Confidence in this Area Using P.A.T.

P _____

A _____

T _____

12

A Walk from Mirrors to Windows

ॐ

The level of life's accomplishments has a lot to do with *where* we look. When looking for what life has to offer and what God has to offer, you must be cognizant of the sources that you use. Let's take a look at two familiar objects that surround us daily: a mirror and a window. The mirror represents our reflections; whereas, the window represents our opportunities. When we look into a mirror, we see our reflections, what's around us, and what's behind us. Mirrors limit what we see. If you've ever just stared at yourself in the mirror, you may notice flaws or imperfections. You may begin to think about all the negative and positive things that happened in your past and how that has shaped who you are. However, you only get to see your replica, what's behind you, or right beside you. This is not much. Your views are limited. Because looking into a mirror shows what's behind you, mirrors can be seen as a reflection of your past events (what happened to you); what you experienced; your regrets and mistakes, etc. However, mirrors can also reflect on your current situations because it shows a replicate of you (what you look like), where you are currently positioned in life, and what surrounds you. Before I possessed confidence and realized the fullness of *who* I am in Christ, I sometimes looked at my reflection in the mirror and asked myself, "Who am I?" My mirrored response to myself was:

> I'm somebody that's kidding myself to think I'm really going to be successful. I'm somebody who may not even graduate college. Besides, no one else in my family received a bachelor's or master's degree. Who am I? I may not make it all the way. I must have forgotten where I come from. I come from a poor family whose dad was a drug addict and alcoholic. My brothers were in and out of prison and the girls in my family all had babies as a teenager (including me). Who am I kidding? I'm from the hood. People from the hood don't make it out like that.

I allowed Satan to feed me those negative thoughts because I saw my life as a mirror only reflecting who I was then, my situation at that point, and what I had experienced in my past.

I saw myself, everything directly around me and directly behind me. My views were limited. Many times, we knock ourselves down, reminding ourselves of our past mistakes or current circumstances.

We don't realize that our perceptions from the mirror (our reflections of past failures, hurt, shame, abuse, etc.) can actually hinder us. If we focus on our mirrors too long, what began as a simple action or thought quickly becomes a powerful stronghold that chains us to our past and dominates our present.

Too often, our views are limited because we see ourselves as we *currently* are instead of what God is grooming us to be. However, my Diva sister, God doesn't see us as we are. He sees us as we're *going* to be! You must start perceiving yourself as God does. God doesn't see your mistakes, blemishes, or setbacks. He sees your remarkable growth, your beauty that He will give in exchange for your ashes, your oil of joy that He will give in place of your heartache, and your triumphant comebacks (see Isaiah 61:3). God doesn't limit you, so you must not limit yourself! Don't focus on your mirror of reflections too long as this can stunt your progress. Mirrors only include where you *were* and where you *are*; however, your focus must be on where you *are going*—your windows.

Surprise naysayers with the results of your success.

All of the statistics that you see throughout this book are predictions of how people view you or how your life is *supposed* to turn out based on your education, your background, your parent's background, your upbringing, etc.

If your parents divorced or were never married, statistics say you're supposed to have constant drama with men or never be able to get married.

If you come from a family where your father, brother, or other family members were inmates in prison, they believe that you will fall right into the category of never amounting to anything in life.

In short, they predict a problematic future for you based off your background, your family, or your past.

~

Women who have babies outside of marriage are
52% more likely to live below the poverty line
and 35% more likely to receive food stamps than
women who had babies
while married. [1]

You Are Not Your Circumstances

When I became pregnant in high school, so many people hoped for my demise. I could literally hear the snickering of some of the girls at my school. Several of the girls talked about me behind my back.

Their mistake was that they saw me *then*; how I was under weather and in a storm *then*. They didn't see my future forecast! The same rings true for you. You aren't able to see the weather forecast by looking at your reflections in a mirror. Only when you look out of the window can you see the sun shining; but people won't give you a window, they will only hold a mirror up to your face to keep your views limited.

One girl told me to join the club of being a teen mother on welfare. But I didn't want to *adjust* to the lifestyle of being on welfare and staying in a town where I could not prosper. Don't get me wrong. I love my small hometown. But, I knew that there was no life there for my child and me. I had a vision regardless of how bad my situation looked. You see, my dream was bigger than my dilemma and that made a world of difference! How big is your dream? How big is your dilemma? When you change your source from your mirrors of reflections to your windows of opportunities, you will be able to dream past, above, and beyond your dilemmas.

The thing I want you to see is that people will always try to put you in some kind of box where there are no other options.

I refused to stay in a box where there were no windows!

It was dark in that box. So dark that I couldn't see hope if I had a flashlight. People will try to give you a mirror and make it seem that all you have are your reflections to rely on.

My reflections showed what I had experienced and who I was *at that time*. My reflections showed that I was broken, scorned, full of mistakes and pain, and even sometimes lost. Even worse, my mirror showed that I was a great candidate for being just another statistic!

My reflections (my mirror) showed that I fit the statistic of the whopping 75% of *teenage* mothers who are poor and forced to live off welfare in their adulthood. [2] I also fell right into the devastating statistic that less than 2% of *teen* mothers earn a college degree by the age of thirty. [2] Moreover, my mirror reflected single motherhood for me because statistics verify that 80% of fathers do not marry the mother of their child. [2]

To the women who encouraged single motherhood on me, to the many people who rejected me, and to all the uneducated, young girls who spoke maliciously of me—to them, I was just a statistic! Do I blame them? Absolutely not; instead, I smile from within because although it is true that my mirror reflected those statistics, they didn't see my windows! The world said I was just a statistic. But God said, I'm a statistic breaker! And so are you! It's not too late to break the chains of statistics off your life.

~

Victims of child sexual abuse are more likely to be sexually promiscuous; More than 75% of teenage prostitutes have been sexually abused. [3]

My mirror predicted a life on welfare, with no college education, and living paycheck to paycheck. My past sexual abuse predicted that I should be addicted to drugs or promiscuous. It predicted that all three of my kids should be fatherless. According to my mirror, I should be with a man who misuses me, or one who impregnates me three times without even marrying me. My reflections of sexual abuse, teen pregnancy, drug abuse, and exposed gang violence gave this forecast for my future. However, I was determined to be something great in life. I turned away from the box with no windows and turned to a window with abundant opportunities. And this has made all the difference! When God sets you up to live an abundant life, nothing else matters. Not your past, not statistics, strongholds, or even your naysayers! This is why you cannot focus on your mirrors or the naysayers. God can and will make your enemies your footstool.

Not only this, but *God can and will make your past your path for your prosperity.* I was determined to beat every odd and to break every statistic. And I did!

Ninety-eight percent of teen moms do not receive a college education by the age of thirty.

There I was: twenty-one years old with a bachelor's degree and twenty-four years old with a master's degree! I received my doctorate degree at the age of thirty-one! Talk about breaking away from statistics!

I am a part of the small 25% of teen mothers who do not need to depend on welfare assistance of any kind. Out of the 80% of men who don't marry the mothers of their children, here I am happily married to the father of all of my children for over twelve years. The list goes on and it was all because at some point, I traded my mirrors in for my windows because windows represent opportunities. My anointed marriage to my husband, my career and college degrees, my financial stability, my blessed children, the gorgeous house that we own, our luxury cars, my successful Book Publishing company and Counseling practice, the DIVAS Unchained Movement, and other ministries are all evident that it was God who favored us. It is due to nothing that we did of ourselves. Glory belongs to God and Him only. *Your future success depends on your walk with God, your vision for your life, and how you respond to life's circumstances.*

I am not ashamed of *anything* from my past! And I mean not a thing! I'm not ashamed of the alley we once lived in, the food stamps we received from the government, my father's drug addiction, or my brothers' incarcerations; nor am I ashamed of my teenage pregnancy, my mistake of who my baby's father was, or the STDs that I contracted.

Once I stopped looking in my mirror and stopped focusing on the reflections of my past pain, I found my windows! **God used my windows to show me that the secret that I was keeping was not my secret, it was my daddy's secret! The sin that was committed was not my sin, it was my daddy's sin! The shame that I was bearing was not my shame, it was my daddy's shame!**

My mirrors didn't allow me to see this because it only showed the reflections of my past and current situations. My windows showed opportunities of freedom and restoration! Once I walked away from my mirrors and into my windows, I received so much peace and joy. I was able to walk as a victor who had conquered the unimaginable; free of shame!

Not only that, God turned it *all* around for my good! You see, if I had stayed in my victim state, I would not have reaped the abundance within my career, joy, family, ministry and finances that I have now because I would have remained stuck; looking at my reflections instead of seeing the opportunities that were ahead of me. This is why you must stop seeing yourself only as you are *now*; you must change your views from the mirror to the window.

My pain taught me endurance and strength.

My upbringing taught me humility.

And the reflections of my mirror taught me pride.

God redeemed me from my past. And you too!

When Jesus shed His blood and rose again, you became free from whatever circumstance that has been keeping you chained. Whether it is the ghetto, drugs, alcohol, unexpected pregnancy, guilt from an abortion, bad relationships, lack of confidence, family drama, illnesses, domestic violence, neglect, poverty, or abuse, you are free from the burdens of it all! Although Jesus made me free from the bondage of my past, the fact still remains that my past helped to make me who I am today. It was God who molded me. I fervently thank God for what I've been through in my life. I would not be able to appreciate life so much if it were not for all of my trials and tribulations.

So, do not let yourself or anybody else define your future based on your past. You are not your past!

Break from those chains today by walking to your windows and seeking God to show you the vast amount of opportunities that await you! You are not even your current circumstances!

You are a *Diva* with vision!

We all have a mirror because we all have a past. But the good news is that we all have a window because we all have a promising future! Declare today that you will walk from your mirrors to your windows. Declare that you are going to be more than what statistics predict about you! Speak that you will go farther than what your situation reflects! Proclaim now (in the name of Jesus) that you are free from Satan's strongholds! You are more than a statistic!

The Stronghold of a Poverty-Stricken Mind

Today, I see too many people living in psychological poverty. Simply put, these are people with a poverty mindset. They feel like they can never be anything more than what their current situation is. Never let your past define your path! Just because you were brought up in a poor neighborhood doesn't mean you have to be chained to that lifestyle. Psychological poverty is when people think that they must be poor all their lives because it's all they know. It's what they are familiar with. Listen: just because someone may be poor doesn't mean their minds and visions have to be poor. A poverty-stricken mindset is a stronghold of the devil. It's one of Satan's tactics to keep you down and out. Those with a poverty mindset never even envision themselves in a nice house because everyone around them have always lived in houses that were raggedy or run-down. They never envision going to college. They think, "That's not what we do in this family. That's not for us."

I remember helping my friend with her college assignments. This friend told me, "When I graduated high school, the thought of going to college didn't even occur to me. But I don't know why."

The wrinkled eyebrows, the raise of her upper lip, and the slow shaking of her head all indicated just how perplexed her thoughts were at that moment. She was really trying hard to figure out why it had taken her two decades to realize that she could do this! She could go to college and get a college degree. Immediately, the wisdom of God within me affirmed this was the result of *psychological poverty*.

Just because someone may be poor doesn't mean their minds and visions have to be poor.

Most times, the thought of going to college never even crosses the mind of a person living in psychological poverty because it's out of the picture for them. They don't see it happening around them or in their circle. College wasn't the *norm* of what happened around her. No one in my friend's family had graduated college, so her views were limited.

She was looking in the mirror which showed her reflections and the things around her.

Many women with a poverty mindset rarely envision marrying a man with a great job, who provides for them and respects them because they are used to abusive or unfaithful men with no jobs or values. They desire a man who cherishes them, but the truth of the matter is that their father cheated on their mother or their uncle abused their aunt, or maybe their sister's boyfriend provides for her sister with drug money. This is what they see, so this is all that they believe is out there for them. Then, there are women and girls who observe the kind of man who protect and provide for the woman and her kids, *but he doesn't cherish her*. Lastly, but not all inclusive, they see the man who really loves his girlfriend or wife, *but won't work a job to save his life*. Women and girls pay attention to all the different kinds of men that are around them; consequently, those men become the norm for what they begin to expect from a man.

Therefore, they *settle* for a man who has at least *one* trait of the package: they compromise their self-worth for either provision **or** cherishment (not both); either leadership **or** protection (not both); either sex **or** love (not both); either love **or** loyalty (not both). They never even envision a man with the total package because they're looking in the mirror reflecting on what's around them instead of looking toward their windows for opportunities of greatness.

So what happens when a lady has a poverty mindset? She doesn't have a vision. She doesn't see herself being more, doing more, or receiving more in life. She may reflect on herself, her environment, and her past when looking in the mirror, but she

৪৯

If we focus on our mirrors too long, what began as a simple action or thought quickly becomes a powerful stronghold that chains us to our past and dominates our present.

never walks to her window. Most of the time, she doesn't even know a window exists for her because she's in psychological poverty. She cannot see or think past her current situation. She's only looking in her mirror, so her views are *limited*.

Without a vision, a woman's sense of self depreciates. A woman with a depreciated sense of self doesn't see her full potential or God's abundant will for her life. Therefore, she cannot perceive her value to society, herself, or God's Kingdom. This is Satan's plan—for women to lack purpose, vision and value.

The Windows of Opportunity

On the contrary, when you look through a *window*, you are able to see far more than what's in your immediate view. You no longer see what's behind you. You see what's in front of you; and what is in front of you is far greater than any mirror is capable of capturing. You are able to see the trees, people, birds, and houses.

Moreover, Ms. Diva, when you look through a window, you are able to see the sky above and the road ahead. This makes all the difference!

My dear *Diva* sister, I admonish you to reflect on your past only to praise God and to be empowered, but don't become fixated on it. The Bible even tells us that at some point, we must stop focusing on the things behind us so that we can focus on our goals ahead and the rewards that God has for us (Philippians 3:13-14). My progress and prosperity came when I ran to my windows! If I had exclusively looked at my mirrors, I would have been stuck in the moments of isolation, shame, and hurt from my past sexual abuse, teen pregnancy, upbringing, etc. Had I only looked at my mirrors, I would not have been able to focus on the things ahead. God had so much more in store for me. I'm reaping the harvest God promised me because I sought Him when walking to my window! Your window is where you see all the opportunities that God has for you. Your window is where you see the sky above. You know that the sky is the limit to what you can do and to what God has planned for you. Your window is where you are able to view the road ahead and see that there is a different road waiting on you to tread; the road to success; the road to prosperity. I assure you that God has a plan for you Ms. Diva. However, Satan wants you to feel like you are stuck. Satan wants you to believe that the chains cannot be broken. This is a stronghold—to keep you feeling like you are bound to a box with mirrors and no windows.

What's in your windows of opportunities?

You must see it!

You've got to envision it! At some point, you've got to stop reflecting on your past and current situations (the mirror) and start focusing on your future and the opportunities that are out there for you (the windows). Don't let your actions stop at your reflections in the mirror! You must take action by walking to a window and seizing all the opportunities that God has in store for you. No matter what part of town you come from, what kind of dysfunctions your family has, what calamities you have experienced, or what obstacles you currently have, sky is the limit to what you can obtain! Choose not to be limited by your mirrors. Choose to be empowered by your windows!

13

Write the Vision

❧

I f you could have any dream to come true in your career life, what would it be? If you could have one dream to come true in ministry, what would it be? How about in your current or future finances? What about your family life? Think for a second…If money, time, resources, or power were not an issue, what would your dreams or goals be? In this chapter, we will discuss your *vision* in relation to your goals and desires. In order to be successful, you must first have a vision. Too many people try to achieve things without a plan. Let's look at the definition of vision. The dictionary [1] defines vision as: "(A) sight; (B) the act or power of anticipating that which will or may come to be—prophetic; or (C) an experience in which a person, thing, or event appears vividly…in the mind…not actually present…under the influence of a divine agency." Now that we have defined vision, I will discuss what I call the "Four steps of the *Vision Process*".

Vision Process Step One
See the Vision

You must first be able to visualize what it is that you want in life. Do you want to graduate college? You must be able to picture yourself graduating college *regardless* of your current situation. When I was pregnant in high school, I was aware of all the odds against me. However, many times I pictured myself being in college and walking across the stage. I saw it.

Do you have a dream of owning a business?

Well, picture it. Let the perfect scenario play out in your mind over and over again without worrying about any obstacles. Visualize the environment, your office, your employees, and your customers.

Do you desire to have a great family one day? Envision it!

What will your husband be like?

Where will you and the children live?

Don't worry about the fact that no one in your family has had the dream family that you want.

Will life always turn out exactly the way you envisioned it? No. However, this is the first step in trusting God to bring your vision into fruition.

After you visualize your dreams and goals, you have turned your dreams into a vision.

Vision Process Step Two
Speak the Vision

After you visualize your goals and dreams, it's time to speak it! The way to do this is to say it aloud and declare it through prayer. Talk to God all about your vision. Keep in mind when you pray that your will must line up with God's will. God says

He will give you the desires of your heart if you delight yourself in Him (Psalm 37:4). You must rearrange your life so that it pleases God. Furthermore, you must be *in love* with God and seek to know more about Him. Once we seek God's face on a daily basis to learn more about Him, we begin to see our desires line up with God's desires for our life. We begin to see that our visions are actually *God's* visions; thus, God's visions become our visions.

Vision Process Step Three
Write the Vision

After you pray to God and tell Him your vision, it's time to write the vision. Write down what God has given you: the desires, goals, and visions. I have a composition notebook specifically for the visions that God has given me. I encourage you to buy a notebook for your visions and write down everything that the Lord has given you. If you have a plan for the way the vision will play out, write it. If you know the people that you would like to be involved with it, write it down. If you have a vision to go to college, write down what you want to major in, when you'd like to go, which college you'd like to attend, and where you'd like to live while attending college.

The Bible says to "Write the vision and make it plain..." (Habakkuk 2:2). Although you will have your own vision, always seek God's command and His further instructions. When this happens, it all begins to flow together.

Always write down the vision exactly the way God gives it to you and write it as clearly as you can.

When God gives you a vision, never deviate from His plan.

Always write down *everything* the Lord gives you concerning that vision. Absolutely *everything* the Lord gives you is very essential in turning your vision into a success.

Writing down the vision the Lord gives you helps to do three things. First, it ensures accuracy of God's instructions. Secondly, it serves as a tool to refer to as you proceed with the vision. Thirdly, it serves as evidence of God's fulfilled promise once He brings your vision to life.

God cannot lie and the Bible tells us that His promises will never return void. If He said it, He'll do it. God says if He speaks a word or a vision, He will certainly bring it to pass. If He gave a plan, He will carry it out (Isaiah 46:11).

Writing the vision serves as evidence to you and others of God's power and provisions. As you look back on the written visions, you will be able to check off everything that God has made happen. Writing the visions allows you to count your blessings and trust God to do even greater things in your life. As I look back over the visions that God has brought to pass, it just gives me more to praise God about. Additionally, it makes it so much easier to leave things in God's control and reduce stress in my life.

Vision Process Step Four
Watch the Vision

Many times, people receive a vision from God and they don't know what steps to take. Other times, people receive a vision from God, pray about it and write it down; however, they fail to *wait and watch* for the vision. Sometimes, God doesn't move when we want Him to move. Everything is done in His own deity and His own time. He knows the right season for your vision to manifest. As stated in Ecclesiastes Chapter 3, there is a time for everything. Therefore, you must watch for the vision to play out and become reality.

In step three, we discussed the scripture Habakkuk 2:2. Let's move on to Habakkuk 2:3 where it states, "For the vision is yet for an appointed time, but at the end, it shall speak and not lie; though it tarries, wait for it; because it will surely come, it will not delay." This is where faith kicks in. You must remember that God's word is truth! If He gave you a vision, it's going to manifest at the right time. It will not be late!

You must stay in prayer about your vision and *watch* for it to happen. If you pray about getting a specific job with specific pay, watch for it. Be on the lookout for the job to post. Sometimes, God speaks through people, places, and things to answer our prayers. He will even speak through the birds. You have to *watch and pray* so that you won't miss what God has in store for you.

Begin to expect things out of God! He wants you to! Wake up in the morning and expect your blessing!

Go to work or school and expect your miracle! Go to bible study and look for your answer.

Go to Sunday morning worship and watch for your breakthrough! It's yours at God's appointed time!

Expect it! Continuously pray for it! *Watch* for it! Then, after you receive it, praise God for it!

Results of the Vision Process

I had a dream of having a career where I helped struggling students stay in high school and help them achieve their high school diploma. This vision of mine came from my desires and passion. I wanted to help the kids that other people had given up on. I wanted to work with those who were pregnant, teen moms, girls and boys that skipped more classes than they attended, the ones with grade point averages of 1.5 and below, etc. I wanted to help them get back on track to graduate. I wanted it to be my actual career where I was paid a comfortable salary because I would live and breathe this career!

This job did not exist!

However, I followed *step one* of the vision process and I **"saw" the vision.** I visualized myself doing everything that I just described. I visualized the career that I wanted many years ago. I will never forget seeing myself as Graduation Coach before that position even existed. How is that so? I saw myself in a counselor-type position (I didn't want to be an actual guidance counselor.) I visualized myself being able to counsel students one on one through advice, activities, and other interventions. I *saw* myself helping to decrease the drop-out rate in schools.

With regards to step two, I **spoke the vision.**

I prayed about it to God and told Him the exact type of job that I wanted. I claimed it! That's right, I claimed a job that didn't even exist! That's how confident I am in God. I did not know how in the world it was going to happen; but nevertheless, I prayed to God about it. My vision was to dramatically improve the lives of students in their education and personal lives while equipping them with the tools to overcome those life's *lemons*. I spoke it boldly into the atmosphere and to God that I was going to have this career providing innovative intervention that worked!

Afterward, I proceeded to step three and **wrote the vision** step by step.

I wrote down the target group for the students that I wanted to work with, the criteria that would make them eligible to receive my assistance, and the methods I would use to assist them. I continued to pray even after I had written the vision down.

Lastly, **I watched for the vision**.

I looked everywhere for an opportunity to come available while continuing to pray and believe. After a year, there it was! It was a position for a Graduation Coach. When I saw the title, I assumed it was just related to helping out at graduation. However, because I was open-minded and watchful, I scrolled down and saw that it was a counselor-type position that required only a teacher's license. I would have missed this if I had not *watched* for the vision to play out. I looked at the job duties and they matched my vision *exactly*. It had the salary that I asked God for as well as the hours and the duties. I was overjoyed! I could not believe it. This was a brand new position that was created by the State in order to increase graduation rate and decrease drop-out rate.

This was a position that did not even exist when I began my vision process! I realized that God had designed that job just for me! It was a custom-made blessing with only my name on it! The victorious success came because I saw it, spoke it, wrote it, and watched for it. God gave me *exactly* what I envisioned! How great is our God! Take your goals, dreams, desires, and *See* the vision, *Speak* the vision, *Write* the Vision, and *Watch* for the Vision!

VIRTUE FOUR

The 'A' In DIVAS

ACHIEVEMENT

"Something that has been done or achieved through effort: a result of hard work; an accomplishment."

Key Bible Scripture

"Beloved, I wish above all things that you may prosper and be in health, even as your soul prospers."

~III John 1:2

14

Nothing Comes to Sleepers But a Dream

༜

The year was 2010. I was in my last semester of graduate school. My goal was to receive my Master's Degree in Education. My obstacles were my marriage issues, my complicated pregnancy, and my responsibilities of being a full time mom of two children and a full-time employee at the college. My options were to quit graduate school and settle with my bachelor's degree or to push through and earn my Master's Degree. I had a decision to make that would significantly affect my life. There is a process for achieving any goal in life. Achievement is "something that has been done or achieved through effort: a result of hard work" (Merriam-Webster Dictionary). When I consulted the Holy Spirit to help me put into words the process of achieving a goal, the acronym *G.O.O.D.* is what I received. For the Divas Unchained, the word *good* stands for Gains, Obstacles, Overcomers, & Decision. You first begin by having a goal in mind that you want to achieve. Use your goal to follow the *G.O.O.D. Achievement Process*:

Gains

If there is an achievement to obtain, there are advantages that come along with it. In this first step of the *G.O.O.D. Achievement Process,* you list all the benefits that you would gain from achieving the goal. The benefits could be things such as working better hours, gaining a sense of fulfillment, securing a better future for yourself and your family, better pay, less stress, etc.

Obstacles

With every goal, you are faced with obstacles. There is always something that will stand in your way of achieving your goal. The obstacles could be that you don't have enough money, you have an illness that causes you to be absent a lot, you have children and no childcare, your friends or family members are unsupportive, etc. Whatever it may be, know that obstacles are inevitable. Obstacles will **always** be in your way. So, now that you know this, what are you going to do about it? It is extremely important that you are aware of every obstacle that could possibly stand in your way. Even before you approach your goal, begin to think about things that could become obstacles. Listen: Be aware of the obstacles, but don't be intimidated by them. God did not give us the spirit of fear; but of power, love and a sound mind (2 Timothy 1:7). You have the power to combat any and all obstacles through God!

Overcomers

Overcomers are the *sacrifices* that you make in order to defeat or conquer the obstacles. Essentially, all God's children have the power to be overcomers. "In all these things we are more than conquerors through him that loved us" (Romans 8:37). Because the obstacles are usually complicated, distracting, tough, and tiresome; you have the power—through Christ, to conquer the obstacles. *Overcoming the obstacles will almost always require sacrifices.* These sacrifices will most likely hurt us in some way. Some sacrifices may cause you to lose sleep, struggle financially for a while, minimize leisure activities, lose social time, and more. You must consider all your options to see whether they are favorable or not.

Decision

After you've weighed in on the gains, recognized possible obstacles, and the different methods of overcoming them, it's time for you to make a decision. Check to see if the gains outweigh the obstacles. Also, check to see if the sacrifices that you must overcome are feasible for you. Using the *G.O.O.D.* Achievement process, my goal was to earn my master's degree. Although God had blessed me to receive a bachelor's degree a few years prior, I had the desire to go further in life and I felt like God was leading me in that direction.

When the Gains Outweigh the Overcomers

You see, I realized that my sacrifices/overcomers were short term while my gains were long-term. If I had given up on my goal, I may not have ever achieved it. Obstacles are *sure* to come. However, you must seek God for ways to overcome those obstacles and weigh them against the gains. Many times with college, if a person keeps putting it off, it never happens. The reason is that life will always get in the way. Your job will become priority because you have bills to pay and probably little mouths to feed. I chose not to allow life's obstacles to defeat me.

God has plans to prosper you in all that you do; He has plans to give you a successful future (Jeremiah 29:11 NIV). You just have to learn to do it God's way—pray for direction and use the *G.O.O.D. Achievement Process* to make sure the gains outweigh the obstacles and that the overcomers/sacrifices are reasonable.

Allow me to enlighten you my sister: **Goals have no power when they are only dreamed; the power comes along when they are in route of being achieved!** I don't encourage anyone to become psychotic by trying to do too much. Remember to make sure that your methods of overcoming obstacles are realistic. I encourage you to achieve your goal by making sacrifices and prioritizing. I felt led by God to go for it because He had more in store for my life. As a result, I made sacrifices. I gave up on hanging out with friends and family for the time being. I chose to quit my job to complete my internship as a graduate student. I am not instructing you to quit your job because everyone's situation is different. However, big sacrifices must be made sometimes. Your sacrifice may not be your job; it may be something else. My husband was very supportive of my decision and he chose to take on a second job to cover all of our bills and expenses. Of course, this left me with the difficult obligation of handling the bulk of the responsibilities with the children. I was accustomed to my husband and me splitting the responsibilities 50-50 with the kids. This had to change so that he could work two full-time jobs. I knew the challenge I was getting into, but I chose to deal with it. I lost so much sleep that I barely had enough energy to eat. I chose to make these sacrifices to achieve my goal: to receive my master's degree. It was so difficult on me that I gave up every day! On the next page is a sketch of my *G.O.O.D.* Achievement Chart.

GOAL: To Receive My Master's Degree

Gains	Obstacles (Current & Foreseen)	Overcomers (My Sacrifices)	Decision
Break statistics placed on those from single parent homes	My Marriage Trials	Postpone some of my volunteer responsibilities	
Create a future for myself and my children	Full time Job: HR Assistant Manager	Say no to many of the night outs with my family	
Receive a higher salary	Full time Job: Mother of two	Quit job and cut back on shopping and eating out	
Become more financially stable	Pregnancy Complications	Lose much sleep Cry many nights	
Option of being home with my children in the summer	Church & Community Commitments	Cut back on television & social networks	Go for the Master's Degree!
Fulfill my passion		More responsibilities with all three kids while husband works second job	**Plan:** Push through and struggle financially and physically through the last three months of Grad School internship
Set milestones for my children to follow			**Reasons:** My gains outweighed my obstacles. My methods of overcoming the obstacles were very hard & required a lot of sacrifice, but were doable.

Read a snippet of the song, "Get Up" by *Mary Mary* [1] below:

> *Layin' Low. Rest n' pause.*
> *Sleeping long. Slow motion*
> *Gonna do, Shoulda, coulda, woulda done*
> *Excuses. What are you afraid of?*
> *Don't you know what you're made of?*
> *One of God's greatest creations*
> *Take this invitation now. Get Up. 'Cause you can't stop*
> *Got a lot to do. 24 hours, Almost gone.*
> *Don't sit there. Get up!*

Before I wrote out the above chart for the *G.O.O.D. Achievement Process,* I was sitting on the couch in my living room with my giant eight-month pregnant belly. I was supposed to be on my way to the school where I was scheduled to complete my internship. I sat on that couch and cried a river! At this particular moment, I had literally given up! I wanted to crawl in a black hole and stay there. My mind was made up. I was going to quit grad school even if I was just within three months of earning my master's degree. I felt I could not go on. This pregnancy was a very difficult one. I was in pain a lot. There were some complicated things in my marriage that I was dealing with. My kids were very young and could not do much on their own. I was definitely depressed.

I thought, "What other decision do I have other than to quit school?"

I cried so much that the top of the dress I had on was soaked.

I felt like life could not get any worse.

Since I was spiritually too weak to pray for myself, I decided to turn the radio on. The song that came on was Mary Mary's "Get Up". [1] The words stuck to me like Velcro. I remember dragging myself out of that bed every day. I felt like if only I had not been pregnant or if only I did not have the marriage problems going on, then I could have gone on with graduate school. But for now, I must stop. At that moment, I heard these words to the song:

> *"Sleeping long...Slow motion...Gonna do, Shoulda, coulda, woulda done...Excuses, what are you afraid of? Don't you know what you're made of? One of God's greatest creations...Get up."*

Then, I thought to myself how much I had been in slow motion and sleeping long, waddling in my issues and depression instead of getting up. I thought about all the times I said I was going to wait until next semester and how I would've been able to go forth with my internship only if my situation was different. I then heard Mary Mary remind me that I am one of God's greatest creations! I was reminded that all things are possible

🙞

The problem is we have too many sleepers, too many dreamers, and not enough achievers.

through God who strengthens me. I was trying to operate off of my own strength rather than the strength of God. The Bible tells us that God's grace is sufficient for us and His strength is made perfect in our weaknesses (2 Corinthians 12:9). I remembered *who* needed to be in control of my situation. And that was God. Of course, my situation said that I could not make it; however, my faith said that I was a conqueror through Christ Jesus. The following words from the song [1] resonated in my head:

> *Welcome to the rest of your life...You've been down too long but now it's time to Get Up...Cause you can't stop. Get up... You got a lot to do. 24 hours almost gone. Get up if you wanna get there. Get Up. Clocks don't stop and Time won't wait.*

I sought God for advice. That's when I realized the power of making sacrifices. I wrote out my *G.O.O.D. Achievement Process* and decided to quit my job, finish pursuing my Master's degree, and allow God to do the rest. This happened only as a result of seeking God for something to be done about my dreams, goals, and desires. I had to get up! No one else could've done this for me and I couldn't blame anyone else for my *should've, could've,* and *would'ves.* It was up to me! God spoke through Mary Mary on this day and made me realize that obstacles will always be in the way. However, time was not going to wait until my marriage got back to where we wanted it. Clocks would not stop just for my hectic life. I had to figure out a way to overcome my challenges. That way was for me to let one of my stressors go even if it meant losing income for a few months. I realized that losing income and struggling for a few months would work out for a greater outcome in the long run for my family and me. On this day, I got up, pursued my master's degree, and achieved it. I cried many days after making this decision. Some days I even gave up again; then, I would go to bed, wake up, and get back in the race all over again. Every time I felt like giving up, I played this song repeatedly. I fervently prayed to God for His strength to be activated instead of my own strength.

I want to encourage you to wake up!

It's time to stop dreaming.

It's time to stop sitting. If the chapters on vision taught you anything, it should be that you must wake up and do something about your dreams. You cannot sleep on your goals. I am a witness that in order to achieve something, you must stop dreaming and wake up.

In order to achieve, you must put in the work. We know that God has all power; but again, faith without action is useless (James 2:17 NLT). Working hard includes sacrificing. Any time you sacrifice, it causes you to hurt in some way, whether it is financially, emotionally, or physically. When I was in college, I lost a lot of sleep. It was a major sacrifice. I was tired all the time, but I got through it. Now that I have my career, I don't have to lose sleep anymore. I don't have to struggle financially anymore. It won't be easy, but anything worth having is worth working hard for. You just have to face the fact that it will cost you in some kind of way. My mother always says "Nothing is truly free but Jesus and salvation." A lot of people have dreams. They dream of being rich, buying their own land, owning their own businesses, etc. Nothing is wrong with having a dream; the dilemma is you only dream when you're in sleep mode or at a standstill. How can anything get done being still or asleep? What happens after you awake from the dream is what matters most. The problem is we have too many sleepers, too many dreamers, and not enough achievers. "Nothing comes to sleepers but a dream." [2] Wake up Diva!

15

The Microwave Generation

❧

When I graduated high school and was on my way to college, one of my aunts asked me how long it would take for me to get my bachelor's degree. I told her it would take approximately four years. She screeched, "Four Years? Oh my goodness! You'll be in school forever! No way!" My aunt did not mean this in a bad way. This could have very well discouraged me; however, I realized that if I wanted success and financial security, it was not going to be handed to me. This current generation is being called the "Microwave Generation". This generation has the, "I want it now and I don't want to work hard for it" syndrome. If you put something in the microwave, it cooks quickly and usually requires little to no preparation time. This is how people of today's generation view success. They want results that are quick and easy. Anything that takes a long time and a lot of work is not worth their time and they will not pursue it. Today's generation looks for instant gratification. *Disclaimer: Not everyone in the Microwave Generation is financially reckless and unstable.* When I use the words *you* and *your* throughout this chapter, I am referring to your generation (whatever age group that may be for you). According to an article by Jenesis Magazine [1], your desire for instant gratification is associated with the high tech, fast speed cell phones, text messages, internet search engines, etc. All

Even people who are not college material are still education material.

of the vast technology makes everything easy, instantaneous, and convenient. Just as the cell phones and internet provide easy and quick access, your generation chooses to only pursue things that provide quick and easy access. If it doesn't fit into the quick and easy category, better known as the "Microwave Generation", you don't go after it.

The desire for easy and instant gratification has made this generation lazy, unmotivated, uneducated, and pessimistic.

What do I mean? For many people, college is not even in the picture because it takes four years to obtain a Bachelor's degree, six years (total) to obtain a Master's degree, and a minimum of eight years (total) to obtain a doctoral degree.

Most times, it's not that a person lacks the ability to succeed in college; it's simply because college does not give an instant or immediate result. Please hear me when I say that I do *not* believe that college is for everyone. However, there are so many people that are "college material", but choose to settle for less. They decide on the "Microwave Generation" route because it's easier, quicker, and requires very little effort and sacrifice.

Those that are not college material seem to just give up. It's okay to not be college "material". However, even people who are not college material are still education material. Everyone (who is in their right mind) is education material because everyone has the capacity to become educated in some way. A person who is educated is one who has knowledge, training, or practice beyond the average person (Merriam-Webster Dictionary). This is not restricted to college degrees. A person can educate herself at home by reading and researching things. Likewise, achievement includes things other than college degrees. Achievement can come in the form of opening a business, passing an exam, receiving a promotion, receiving an award, being offered a job, etc. Remember, achievement is anytime you set a goal, work hard for that goal, and accomplish the goal.

You can be well-educated without a college degree.

There are many careers that do not require a four year college degree, but still have very great salaries.

More than 46% of African-American women are employed in low-income jobs. [2]

No Shortcuts

You too, can do what you desire if you stay away from the microwave generation mindset that says, "I want it now and I don't want to work hard for it." Remember, the "Microwave Generation" wants to make a lot of money without spending long hours receiving the training or education for it. You want to drive a nice car without having to build your credit up. All my life, I've seen people who attempt to gain success by taking shortcuts. These are the people that receive a credit card application in the mail for $500.00 and apply for it with no intentions on ever making the monthly payments on the card. They max out the credit card as soon as they receive it by purchasing shoes, rims for their car, tattoos, the latest iPhone, and all kinds of designer purses and clothing. This is because they view their financial success as a shortcut.

There are no shortcuts to genuine achievement.

I want to remind you that the definition of achievement is *a result of hard work.*

Hard work does not include shortcuts.

So unless an outcome is the result of major effort and hard work, it is probably not achievement.

The $500 credit card limit is temporary, but the debt is long-term. This person who received $500 and spent it in less than a week will spend years and years of financial struggles as a result of this shortcut action. Additionally, *quality* car dealers will deny any requests to purchase a nice vehicle. If approved, they will have an extremely high interest rate which adds up to far more than the $500 credit card limit that they maxed out on frivolous things. The same thing applies to purchasing a home... denied a loan or an extremely high mortgage.

Achievement Deficiency

I graduated college one year early with a bachelor's degree. The reason is because I made sacrifices. I thought long-term. Sometimes, I wanted to go to the parties like other collegmates. I wanted to stay out all night, but I couldn't. If I was going to achieve my goal, I could not do what others did. There are many that begin college, but don't finish. What happened? Many times, it's because they didn't make sacrifices. Their priorities were not in order. They wanted the fast track life. They saw what they wanted and they wanted it right away. They did not want to work hard for it. Just like a microwave, they wanted it quickly. They didn't add up the cost. Sometimes, the fastest way is not the smartest way. You must weigh the advantages against the disadvantages. When you make decisions, always think about the long term results.

Think of it this way: the majority of the microwaveable food is packed with excessive sodium and other unhealthy ingredients. The quick and convenient "microwaveable" eating can lead to a *nutritional deficiency*.

The same is true for achievement. If you always shoot for the instant and easy routes to success, the short term benefits may be good to you. However, the long term affects may be detrimental to your success. If you place your focus all on fun and materialistic things more than your achievements, you will undoubtedly develop an *achievement deficiency*.

Micro means small; therefore, microwave thinking is small-minded thinking. In order for you to achieve your goals, you must remove all micro-minded thinking and gain long-term thinking. Don't develop an achievement deficiency by being micro-minded.

Children whose parents are uneducated are approximately 41% more likely to experience poverty in their adulthood than children with educated parents. [3]

An Investment in Your Future

Many people see college as a *waste of time* because, as they say, "College doesn't pay you." There is some truth in this, depending on how you look at it. A *Diva of Achievement* will look at college as an investment in her future which means in actuality, it does pay in the long run and for a long time. Usually, college requires a lot of time. Most people that have graduated college will agree that college is not extremely hard, but it is very time consuming and requires a lot of self-discipline.

The Microwave Generation does not adhere to those two things: they don't want to hear about anything that takes too much of their time and they definitely don't want to commit to anything that they must work hard and sacrifice for. Therefore, obtaining an ordinary job seems *easier and less time consuming* than going to college, gaining a trade, or receiving experience.

Furthermore, a job gives instant gratification which comes in the form of a weekly or bi-weekly paycheck. This paycheck allows a person to meet their needs immediately. On the contrary, college does not give a person a bi-weekly paycheck. Instead of studying, they could be partying, going out to eat with friends, etc.

Any type of education is an investment in your future and in **the future of your children. The few years or months that you spend on your post-high s**chool education will set you up for a lifetime of financial security. This is not to say that it will automatically make you rich. However, it will establish a stable life for you for the rest of your life.

Whatever you obtain: whether it's a degree, license, certification, trade, or skill, believe me that it is far more than just a piece of paper. It is your job security and your financial stability.

People lose jobs every day.

Those with no *piece of paper* find it extremely difficult to obtain another *satisfying* job.

However, your percentages of finding a job substantially increase when you have a post-high school education of some sort. Remember this: They can take your job away; your house can be foreclosed; your car can get repossessed; but no one on this earth can ever take a diploma from you! It is yours to take with you from job to job and state to state.

Speaking of colleges and trades, several people enroll in college solely to receive a refund check. My heart aches for our people when I see this happen. They never have any intention on getting an education; they just see the money as instant and easy. This is a disgrace to your intellect!

It is a *Diva* of Achievement who enrolls in college and actually places energy into college that will help her in the long run. She thinks long-term, not short-term.

When you begin to see education as an investment, you have graduated from the microwave generation mindset.

Again, a four-year college degree is not for everyone. If you have searched your heart and you know it's not for you, no worries! However, find a trade, license, certification, skill, or other business venture to pursue. Make a decision today to stop thinking like the microwave generation and think like an achiever. If you need help finding something suitable for you or someone to help you through the process, pray about it. Consult a Life Coach to assist you. Don't be the one that goes years making statements such as, "I wish I could..." Choose to be more than a dreamer. Choose to be an achiever. With God, all things are possible to *she* that believes!

16

Succeed on Purpose

❦

It was Maya Angelou that said, "I've learned that making a living is not the same thing as making a life." [1] There is a profound difference between a job and a career. The person with a job works in order to live; she works in order to survive. On the contrary, the person with a career is making a life for herself and her family. She is thinking of long term success. A job allows you to earn money, but a career allows you to achieve a goal that you've pursued. A career provides better long term benefits. A person with just a job cannot usually retire comfortably. It could be that the job didn't offer retirement benefits, she couldn't afford them, or the benefits were not enough to retire on. Therefore, the person with a job usually works until her body cannot take it anymore and they must live off social security alone. A person with a career can retire much earlier and receive almost as much compensation as she received when she was working. A career provides stability whereas a job requires many abrupt changes in work hours, locations, duties, etc. A career usually allows for more promotions than a job. A job should be temporary. A career should be long-term. It can be argued that some people have just so happened to *stumble* upon success. For example, the man who discovered the antibiotic penicillin was said to have done so by *accident*.

I once heard one of my students argue, "Success *can* happen overnight because Mark Zuckerberg (Founder of Facebook) meant for his social network to be for the college he attended; but it skyrocketed and went nationwide in no time." For Mark Zuckerberg and the man who discovered penicillin, it can be argued that their outcomes exceeded their initial purpose. However, their brilliance allowed them to succeed in an exceptional way. Many people (such as my former student) want success to happen this way for them. Unfortunately, this is not usually the case.

Having a purpose implies that you *intend* on something to happen; you have a reason for what you are doing, and you aim for a specific outcome. As such, I'm here to argue that **it is crucial that you succeed on purpose rather than waiting and hoping for chance to just happen to you**. The thing with chance is that the risks are high and the opportunities are low. It's like the person that waits his entire life on winning the lottery or the jackpot at the casino. Do you know this type of person? They wait around all their lives spending (or shall I say losing) money at the casino or on lottery tickets. They continue to talk about how rich they will be once they win the lottery while they struggle on a daily basis to make ends meet. Then all of a sudden, years have gone by and they are still in the same position with no money or job security.

What is wrong with this picture? This is the picture of a person who is *waiting* on chance to happen to them rather than *making* success happen for them. The difference is in the words "waiting" and "making". If you want to achieve goals in life, you cannot just *wait* for it to happen. You must *make* it happen. In this chapter, I will provide you with five strategies for success so that you may succeed *on purpose*, not by chance.

Purpose Strategy #1
Educate Yourself

Education is not an option for success; it's a priority. When you get to this point, you are already halfway to achieving your goal. I really like the famous quote by Benjamin Franklin, "If you fail to plan, you are planning to fail." [2] After you have followed the G.O.O.D. Achievement method from a previous chapter, and have made your decision to pursue a goal, it's time to make a plan.

You must have a purposeful plan to become educated. For example, let's say that you are a secretary with a goal of managing a business one day. In order to succeed on purpose, you should purposefully learn everything there is to know about that job even if you do not plan on managing that particular business. Some people think that just because they do not plan on working at the place where they currently are, they should only perform the minimum requirements. That is not so. Ask questions. Take notes on what the other employees and supervisors are doing. Study some of the materials on your own. If there is specific software that they work on, try to gain as much knowledge as possible. In the previous chapter, I informed you that education comes in more forms than one.

Even if you are not in college, you can still educate yourself. Businesses look for people that have a plethora of experience and knowledge in various areas. Choose not to be the person that cannot hold an intelligent conversation with others. You can do something about it! You can educate yourself. I choose not to be ignorant. Ignorance is by choice.

~

About 40% of Black girls fail to graduate high school each year. [3]

That's 4 out of every 10 black girls.

Purpose Strategy #2
Say No to Mediocrity

Allow me to familiarize you with a quote by Gordon B. Hinckley that says, "Mediocrity will never do. You are capable of something better." [4] Ms. Diva, the Godly truth is that **no matter what you've done in the past, what you've experienced, or what your current situation is, you are capable and deserving of something better!** God wants more for you! God is not a settling God! He doesn't want you to settle because He has it all. The Bible tells us that the earth is the Lord's and everything in it belongs to Him (Psalm 24:1). He has the ability to give you anything that you want, but it must line up with His will.

Mediocrity is when you do just enough to get by.

It's when you only do the minimum and settle for less.

Mediocrity is how an average person thinks. It's the way a

dreamer thinks; not an achiever. Mediocrity tells you that you can't and you won't. It tells you that you are not capable to pursue more or that you are not good enough to be more.

Mediocrity is what separates the dreamers from the achievers. Mediocre people stop at dreaming; they don't pursue or achieve the goal. Truth be told, it's not a person's power that enables her to do anything, but the power and strength of God. "For God is working in you, giving you the desire and the power to do what pleases Him" (Philippians 2:13). When you learn to look at it this way, you realize that you must rely on God's power and strength to equip you to do whatever it is that you aspire

Mediocrity is what separates the dreamers from the achievers.

to do. Although we as humans are not always capable of doing certain things due to our current circumstances, God is always able to give us the knowledge, skills, and energy to do things.

He knows just what to do and how to shake things up in order to work out our situations to reach our goals. He knows how to provide resources such as the appropriate people to send your way to help achieve your goal.

If you want to succeed, you must step away from being mediocre. How do you do that? You set high, but reasonable expectations for yourself. If the class you're taking requires you to get a C in order to pass, and you aim for a C, you are in trouble when you receive a grade of 68 in the class. When we set an expectation, sometimes we fall below the bar due to unforeseen circumstances.

This is why you must always set higher expectations for yourself and aim for those expectations. When you set low expectations (or mediocre expectations), you subconsciously train your brain to only aim for that level. However, when you set higher expectations, you train your brain to aim higher. In essence, mediocrity sets you up for failure. It also sends a message that you are not worth more. As stated in the quote earlier, you are more than mediocrity. God says you are. (see Psalm 139:14) Be sure to set high goals, but be realistic and true to yourself.

$$\sim$$

52% of African-American women have a difficult time paying monthly utility bills. [5]

Purpose Strategy #3
Prepare for Roadblocks

The previous chapter urged you to consider obstacles that may come in your way. This must be continuous. You must always *purposefully* prepare for possible roadblocks. When I was in college, I got sick several times from allergies, severe migraine headaches, sinusitis, etc. I chose not to miss classes because I had little kids and I always knew that in the back of my mind, they would get sick which would require me to stay home. I was saving my absent days for the days when I had no choice but to stay home.

I knew that if I stayed home, I would miss lectures and the more days I missed, the further I would fall behind in my work.

I prepared for my roadblocks. Once, my three year old son came down with the flu which required me to stay home for a week. There were numerous things that occurred throughout the years that required me to miss school. Think about if I had stayed home when I was feeling a little under the weather; then, add the days that my children were sick. I would be so far behind to the point of not being able to catch up during the semester. If this continued, I would've probably been a freshman for a second or third time. When this happens, people just drop out because it gets discouraging for them. Many people in this same predicament who drop out of college believe the reason it was difficult to stay in college is because of the babies or other situations; however, oftentimes, it's because they did not prepare for the roadblocks of the children or other situations. You can apply this to any goal that you are trying to achieve. My children's illnesses were not the only roadblocks that I had to endure. Sometimes, a family member was in trouble and I missed a week of classes as a result. I prepared for these *unseen* roadblocks by missing out on my sleep and my outings. There were many times that I was so exhausted, but I stayed up to study because I knew that it was possible that something would come up one day to where I could not study. If you want achievement, you must *prepare for roadblocks on purpose!*

Purpose Strategy #4
Say Yes to Networking

Have you ever heard the saying, "It's all about who you know?" It's true that knowing certain people can help you get your foot in the door and help you achieve much more. If you are in high school, college, or trade school, it's important for you to make connections with your teachers. This means having a positive relationship with your teachers/professors. You will need your teachers in the future because scholarship coordinators, internships, and employers will ask you to obtain recommendation letters from your current or former teachers. If you always have an unpleasant attitude, low participation, or failing academic record, they will not write a letter for you. You should keep an academic portfolio of your accomplishments such as any projects or special essays that you've completed. Volunteer work is very crucial for the networking purpose. It allows you to meet very important people that can have a voice in your future. They can recommend you for a job, career, internship, scholarship, or college just by one simple phone call. Whoever you come in contact with that has high status or great caliber, make sure you hold a decent, intelligent conversation with them. Inform them of your goals and your accomplishments. Many times, they have connections and can help you get started in the right direction. The person I worked for when I was just a work-study student was my mentor. His name is Dr. Robert Mock. He was a great mentor. He mentored me throughout my entire bachelor's degree. He taught me about the different degrees and why it was so important to get a degree with a great job outlook. I even met more professional, successful people because of our mentorship. This is what networking is all about. It is essential that you meet some high-achieving people and gain a professional relationship with them *on purpose*!

Purpose Strategy #5
Choose Appropriate Grammar

"You talk like a white girl!" "Why are you talking all proper?" Girl, you're not white!" These are statements that I've heard all my life. I heard them so much that I tried hard to change the way I spoke. When I matured and became more educated, I realized that there is no such thing as talking *white*. I hear this too much. People tell my son that he talks white. They mean that he enunciates. He pronounces his words accurately.

I'm sure you've heard the "talking white" statement before.

It is a downright insult to our intelligence. Little do our people know that when they say this, they are really saying that we are not capable of the same education as white people. It implies that we are not as intelligent or as worthy as white people. This is so far from the truth! Oh, how Satan deceives our people! Black people are just as capable of learning

Speaking appropriate grammar is not talking white; it's talking educated.

as white people are. Let's stop living up to the stereotypes. I urge you to negate any belief that speaking correct grammar is talking "white". Speaking appropriate grammar is not talking white; it's talking educated.

It is sad that some people only associate correct grammar with white people. That's the mentality of the enslaved. It is even sadder that some people consider correct grammar as a bad thing. Speaking correct grammar is one of the strategies of success. Moreover, it's one of the indicators of an educated person. It is a way to achieve greater things in life.

We are no longer in slavery; so my question is why are our people still using slave language such as "you is" and "I'm is"?

This is the language that our people used because they were *banned* of the right to be educated. Speaking incorrect grammar like this was *their only choice* in slavery. Anyone in slavery is in bondage. The Bible tells us that God did not give us the spirit of bondage, but the spirit of adoption (Romans 8:15). This means that you don't have to live in bondage with your financial situation, relational situation, or your career situation. You became one of God's own adopted children through Jesus Christ. Everything that He has, you have access to it, but you must declare it and tap into it through prayer, faith, and obedience. Refrain from *slave* language and take on the educated language that is available to you and made *free* unto you. According to a blog for Harvard Business Review, if a person sees that you don't think your grammar is important, then you won't think other things are important in the business place. [6]

We all make grammatical mistakes, but why do people purposefully misspell words (yhu for you and dere for there)? Why purposefully choose to reverse every good sense of grammar that they have learned? It is basically throwing the middle finger at our ancestors and saying, "Forget every one of you that cried, fought, and bled for our education rights! I'm going to reverse it all!" Our ancestors fought so that African- Americans can have the right to an education and this is how "we" show appreciation. Someone named Donny Miller once quoted, *"In the age of information, ignorance is a choice."* [7]

God wants you to achieve. He said that He has plans to prosper you and plans to give you hope and a future (Jeremiah 29:11). God doesn't want you to self-diminish your intellect or mental capacity. *If you want to continue to stay in the same place that you are, choose ignorance. However, if you are ready to move forward, choose education!* Leave the naysayers behind because they are not going in the same direction that you are. Remember, you can be educated in ways other than a college degree. Choose to learn something new every day. You can start with your grammar. It is the road to your success and it *can* determine whether you will always have a job or a career. God made you to do more…to be more…to achieve more! Decide on today to *succeed on purpose*!

17

The Greatest Achievement of All

◦

So many very successful people who have it all still find themselves seeking to fill a void—a feeling that something is missing. They search for a long time looking for something to fill the emptiness. All along, the *something* that's missing is their relationship with God. They have everything; however, their body and flesh is fulfilled, but their spirit is not. God wants you to be successful. He is there to help you achieve your goals. It is stated in III John 1:2, "Beloved, I wish above all things that you may prosper and be in health, even as your soul prospers." Ms. Diva, God wants you to prosper and achieve. However, in all your achieving, I urge you to get a spiritual education. A spiritual education is the one that keeps on giving. Not only is it the vehicle to all other achievements; it is the achievement that *sustains* all other achievements. There's a song that says, "When everything else fails, I can go to the rock." That rock is Jesus Christ. God should not be just a piece of the pie in our lives; He should be our foundation to what everything else is built upon. Jesus said, "…Upon this rock, I will build my church and the gates of hell shall not prevail against it" (Matthew 16:18). Anything that is built with Christ as the rock/foundation will *not* be overpowered or destroyed. I urge you to build your house (your family, relationships, finances, career, friends, etc.) on the foundation of Jesus Christ.

Build Your House on a Strong Foundation

Let's just say that you build a house (metaphorically speaking) with several rooms each consisting of your life's achievements. In the different rooms, you have a room called family; a different room called career; one called marriage; a room called ministry; another called friends; one called personal relationships; another called college; one called peace; one called leisure and entertainment, etc. These different rooms make up your house. As with any house, if it does not have a solid foundation, it will shift and eventually crumble.

If a house has a weak foundation, it will crack and crumble with time. You can apply this same principle to your life. The foundation that your spiritual achievement house is built upon can either make the house last forever or cause the house and all of its components to collapse.

The components that consist of a great career, awesome husband and kids, great friends, entertainment life, and ministry can all collapse if Jesus is not the foundation that these things are built upon.

The foundation of your achievement house must be solid.

This means that you must build a relationship with God that

goes beyond going to church out of routine. When you begin a relationship with someone, it means that you and the other person know each other and take time to learn more about each other. You talk to each other all the time. You become best friends, and spend quality time with each other. When someone has your heart, you make them priority and everything else takes the backseat. This is the way to develop a relationship with God. I can attest to this because it has proven to be true in my life. This is also the way to make God the solid foundation of your life.

When you think of a relationship such as that of a boyfriend or even a parent, you make sacrifices for them. You sacrifice your time, sleep, money, and more because of your love for them. This is what God is looking for. This is what the Lord means when He says, "Take delight in the Lord, and He will give you the desires of your heart" (Psalm 37:4 NIV). To delight in someone means to find pleasure in them; to satisfy them; to fall in love with them; and to find joy with them.

God wants you to be interested in Him beyond Sunday sermons. He wants you to have a desire to learn more about him and take interest in Him. Once you do this, everything else will fall into place. If you do this, you don't even have to worry about your needs and desires. God says if He takes care of the birds so that they have no worries, surely He will take care of you, His very own daughter (Matthew 6:25-26).

There's a parable in the Bible about two men who both built houses (see Matthew 7:24-27). One man built his house on sand because it was very easy and quick. He was finished in a very short amount of time.

The other man built his house on a rock which took much longer. As time passed, a very violent storm came upon the houses of both men. The man's house that was built on sand was destroyed and swept away by the flood. On the other hand, the house that was built upon a rock was safe. In the midst of the horrible storm, the house stood: unmoved and unharmed. It took only a short amount of time to build the house on sand; but in the long run, this house was completely destroyed.

On the contrary, the house built on a rock—on a solid foundation—required a longer time to build; but even though the winds and rain beat against the house, it was not overtaken by the storms and floods in the long run. The same applies to your life. Yes, it may require time to develop a healthy relationship with the Lord. However, with Him as your foundation, your house, every component, and every achievement that is a part of your house will be protected from the storms of life even though the rain may fall and the stormy winds may blow.

The key difference between a strong spiritual foundation and a weak spiritual foundation is the daily, conscientious effort a person makes in order to please God. Although we fall short, we are to keep our focus on Godly things and make every effort to stay away from ungodly things. We confess our sins and ask God to forgive us daily knowing that He forgives us immediately upon repentance. This is how we walk in the Spirit. However, the Bible lets us know that we are not supposed to sin on purpose just because we know God will forgive us (Hebrews 10:26).

A change does not usually happen overnight.

The more we walk in the Spirit of God, the more the Holy Spirit changes our behaviors. However, you must continue to walk in the Spirit and not in the *flesh*. The ways of the flesh are the ways of the world. God meant for you to be set apart from the world. Temptations will surely come. However, the Bible tells us the biggest and most powerful weapon is the word of God and prayer. Read your Bible and pray every single day and watch how the Lord moves! Even two or three verses per day can speak to your heart and spirit.

The Bible tells us to hide His word in our hearts (Psalms 119:11). When we read the Bible, God's words are stored in our hearts so that when we go through storms, the Holy Spirit will bring the appropriate scriptures to our attention to encourage us during our trials. If you don't have any of His word in you, how can the Holy Spirit bring it to your attention when needed? I have been so depressed to the point of not wanting to live and right in the nick of time, the Holy Spirit reminded me of scriptures that have been stored in my heart for a long time. It is amazing how much that helps! The Holy Spirit is our help and our comforter! Praying is a two-way street. You talk to God, and then you listen to the Holy Spirit. God speaks to different people in different ways. The more you spend time with God, the more you find out the way He speaks to you. Just like you spend time with a guy to get to know more about him, you must spend time with God to know more about Him.

Here is Jesus' response about the two men who built houses:

> The rain came down, the streams rose, and the winds blew and beat against that house; yet it did not fall, because it had its foundation on the rock. But everyone who hears these words of mine and does not put them into practice is like a foolish man who built his house on sand. The rain came down, the streams rose, and the winds blew and beat against that house, and it fell with a great crash (Matthew 7:24-27 NIV).

Your Lifestyle

Let us be like the man who built his house on a strong, solid foundation so that when storms come in our lives, we will be prepared and protected. I have included some spiritual formulas that will help you better visualize the spiritual foundations. God forgives quickly, but we must repent of our sins (Acts 3:19). Be advised that repentance means to feel apologetic for our sins *and* make a commitment and effort to turn away from our sinful actions.

This is what repentance looks like:

> "If my people, which are called by name, will humble themselves and pray, and seek my face, and turn from their wicked ways; then will I hear from heaven, and will forgive their sin, and will heal their land" (II Chronicles 7:14).

Spiritual Foundation Formula 1

    Much prayer and worship
+ Much Bible reading
+ Much repentance
− A Worldly Lifestyle
= *A Strong Spiritual Foundation*

Spiritual Foundation Formula 2

    Little prayer and worship
+ Little Bible reading
+ Little repentance
− A Godly Lifestyle
= *A Weak Spiritual Foundation*

You see, a Godly lifestyle does not mean that you will do every-thing perfectly. It has more to do with the *daily* walk that you are committed to. A Godly lifestyle is where you practice every day to be free from a particular sin or sins. It's when you ded-icate yourself every day to becoming a new person with God, while taking it one step at a time. A lifestyle is the way that you live on a regular basis. So, now is the time to ask yourself, "How am I living on a regular basis?" **Doing something on occasion or out of tradition does not denote a lifestyle.** If someone randomly visited you for a while, and you acted as usual, what would they see? This is your lifestyle. Now is the time to evaluate your life to see if your spiritual foundation is weak or strong. A lifestyle is what you are defined as. It's also who people see you as. People who know me are familiar with my character. When I asked a friend of mine to tell me about a new good place to eat at night, she responded, "I know of some places, but I don't think you would like them because they are club-like places." She knows that my lifestyle does not consist of going to places like that. I love to have a good time. I love to go different places, but I try to do it all in the light of pleasing God. Do I do things that God doesn't approve of sometimes? Yes, I do. I'm flawed just like everyone else. I repent and try my best to work on them. However, for the most part, my way of living says that I am a woman committed to living for God.

Do not be as the man who built his house with little effort on sand. Because his house was not built on a strong foundation, the storms destroyed it. The storms of life come in the forms of overdue bills, accidents, relationship issues, troubled children, car troubles, foreclosures, repossessions, bankruptcies, deaths, illnesses, depression, loss of jobs, etc.

Storms are surely to come in our lives.

So, I urge you to do as the other man in the story did. Build your house on the rock of Jesus Christ through much prayer and worship, Bible reading, daily repentance, and a Godly lifestyle so that when the storms of life come, your house will withstand the impact. Within the blink of an eye, God has the power to take everything away that a person has achieved.

With that said, He also has the power to give it all back to you, allow you to keep it all, and to add on to what He's already blessed you with. Having a strong spiritual foundation can also help you make life-changing decisions. Although we all make mistakes, those that don't have a relationship with God can make very grave mistakes that can cause them years of distress. God informs those who have a relationship with Him to let our requests be made known to Him through prayer and He will give us peace about the situation and keep us from sinking due to our own actions (see Philippians 4:6-7).

There have been many times that my relationship with God has led me to my continued achievement. When I was on my way to major in Nursing; after praying and seeking the Lord for a while, He made it clear that I was supposed to major in Communication. I made up so many reasons as to why I should not do Communication; however, the Holy Spirit said otherwise. Now, I see clearly the reason for my degrees as I minister with the gift of communication through my inspirational writings and motivational speeches to others. If I had majored in nursing, that would have been a very costly mistake! I knew the way to go because I had a relationship with Him and was able to consult Him and receive direction.

When you have an intimate relationship with God, it's much easier to hear what He is saying to you because you are familiar with the way that He speaks to you. God doesn't want you to treat Him like a long-lost friend whose voice you cannot recognize due to your lack of communication. He wants a continual relationship with you. God doesn't want us to bring sorrow to His Holy Spirit by a worldly lifestyle or our infrequent talks with Him (Ephesians 4:30).

So many people ask me how I became so successful. They see my success, but they don't know what I had to do to get here. It took a lot of sacrifice, tears, pain, hard work, and prayer. The gospel duo *Mary Mary* has a song called "God in Me" [1] that says *"What they don't know is when you go home and get behind closed doors, man you hit the floor, and what they can't see is you on your knees, so the next time you get it, tell them it's the God in me."* In the song [1], they speak of how people see others writing big checks, dressing nice, and living prosperous, but the reason is because of the person's relationship with God through prayer. Many people want prosperity, but they don't want to give God the uninterrupted time. He has so much in store for His children, if only they would seek His face and develop a strong relationship with Him.

When you make Him your priority, "The Lord will guide you continually, and satisfy your soul in drought, and strengthen your bones: and you shall be like a watered garden, and like a spring of water, whose waters fail not" (Isaiah 58:11). This is why a spiritual achievement is the greatest achievement of all. It is an achievement that keeps on giving. It will never fail you. When all else in life fails, God will not (Hebrews 13:5)! Once you accept the Holy Spirit, you will always have it with you to guide you when you don't know what decision to make about life's choices. The Holy Spirit is not only our comforter and help; but John 14:26 notifies us that the Holy Spirit is our teacher. When life lets you down because the company laid you off, your car got repossessed, the childcare fees increased, a relationship failed, a loved one wounded you, or an illness has crept into your body, you need someone to comfort you, give you peace, guide you, and restore all that was lost. That someone is the Holy Spirit: the comforter, the teacher, the intercessor, the gift that keeps on giving, and the well that never runs dry.

You have not completely excelled in life until you have achieved a solid spiritual foundation.

It is the achievement that keeps on giving! The greatest achievement of all is spiritual achievement.

VIRTUE FIVE

The 'S' In DIVAS

SISTERHOOD

"A close relationship among women based on shared experiences, concerns, etc."

Key Bible Scripture

Two people are better off than one, for they can help each other succeed. ~Ecclesiastes 4:9 NLT

18

Your Sister's Keeper or Defeater?

ॐ

Do you want to know how to significantly decrease the female conflict in your life and around you? The best way to keep your name out of drama is to look the other way when someone begins talking negatively about other people. Leave the room if you can. People should not feel comfortable talking about others around you. You don't have to say a word when they speak negatively about other women. You can become an accomplice even if you reply in a certain way. Whether you are the talker or merely the listener, gossip takes two! *"Fire goes out without wood, and fights disappear when gossip stops"* (Proverbs 26:20 NLT). Choose not to be the wood that keeps the fire going. Choose not to be the sister that ignites fights with her gossip. By taking a stand, you can become a pioneer in stopping a destructive cycle of strongholds against sisterhood. All women are our sisters and should be viewed as such. God designed us to be interdependent; to be our sister's keeper. This does not apply only to our biological sisters, but all of our sisters, regardless of race or bloodline. When we negatively gossip about our sisters, we are engaging in defeating them, not keeping them.

"If you suffer, however, it must not be for murder, stealing, making trouble, or prying into other people's affairs" (1 Peter 4:15 NLT). Isn't it amazing that the Bible lists gossiping on the same level as murder and stealing? It is obvious that God views gossip as a serious sin because it brings others down, destroys characters, takes the gossiper's focus off their own important matters, and stirs up wrath, hatred, and therefore, more sin. Black women not only have to deal with the stigma and stereotype from other races, but we must also deal with the double edged-sword from our own kind.

Is it not enough to feel knocked down by others?

Must we as black women continue to go against our own?

Disclaimer: Throughout the next few pages, you will see where I use language such as "We" and "Our". When I say black women in the following pages, I am not referring to every single black woman as we know there are exceptions. As an African American woman, we are in this together. The purpose of these final chapters is to expose and break down the chains of statistics and strongholds that work so powerfully against our sisterhood.

Three Strikes Against Our Sisters

I have come to the conclusion that the reason black women lack sisterhood is a result of the unfortunate disadvantages relative to black women. Women, in general, *regardless* of race, are considered minority when compared to men.

This can be considered as **strike one**.

African American women are also considered minority with regards to Caucasian women.

Let's consider this **strike two**.

Whether it's in the workplace or home, minority women are said to be at a disadvantage. Generally speaking, it is difficult for black women to thrive in our society due to different circumstances. The statistics do not lie. Black women generally suffer from *multiple* strongholds such as single-mother households, imprisoned fathers and sons, physical abuse, sexual abuse, failed marriages, lack of marriages, high rate of babies born out of wedlock, family dysfunction, and a lack of education.

I consider these unfortunate strongholds that plague our black women as **strike three**.

Black women feel cheated, left out, or unworthy.

Generally speaking, the way most black women see it is that most white women possess more than the average black woman, so then it becomes a game of trying to outdo another black woman. After all, what is the need to lash out against white women or try to exceed them? This is seen as a waste of time; therefore, we lash out at other black women.

The unperceived and unspoken truth is that the black women are in the same disadvantage boat as the next; nevertheless, women try to exceed them in an attempt to feel some worth. After all, there are already three strikes against black women; so there is a subconscious belief that they must fight to fit in anywhere that's not last. This is when it becomes a game of being intimidated, envious, spiteful, and competitive toward other black women of our own equivalent. Thus, we have no room to be our sister's keeper due to all the strikes that have invaded us. So after feeling defeated from strikes one through three, we begin striking each other (our sisters) by way of lying, gossiping, backbiting, fighting, envying, etc.

In other words, we kick our sisters down when they are already down by three strikes—being black, being female, and being a victim of specific strongholds.

The Sisterhood Cycle of Defeat

It's actually a sad irony— since we are equals, by fighting our sisters, we are actually fighting ourselves. Every time one black woman knocks another one down, the cycle is repeated and we all know that a cycle comes back around to the beginning at some point. Therefore, the spiteful action comes back on you, is aimed toward you or toward a loved one of yours. Hurt people hurt others. When one sister hurts another sister, *that* hurt sister then hurts *another* sister. Soon, the cycle continues and the hurt through the chain of your previous action toward one sister has now come back against **you** from another sister.

I call this the *"Sisterhood Cycle of Defeat"*. The cycle just keeps repeating. Knock one down. Another gets knocked down. The results? We all stay down. Someone must break the cycle! It must stop *somewhere*!

Rumors are spread from one sister to another. Some women blatantly ambush another sister in public and on social media with the desire to make her ashamed in front of others. They post pictures or send screen shots of text messages to humiliate one another. What has been done for so long is constantly repeated until we are ignorant of Satan's devices to keep the black woman down. The cycle of hurt, hatred, and defeat toward our own sisters (and ourselves) continues because we fail to engage in sisterhood. Because we are equals, all the gossiping, fights, hurt, and attempts to defeat our

ৎৠ

By defeating our sisters, we choose to defeat ourselves!

own sisters create a continuous cycle of *sister*-hatred, but also a continuing a cycle of self-hatred. How so? Because we are all equal. If we cannot respect our equals (our own black sisters), how can we expect others to respect us? By not respecting our equals (our sisters), we choose not to respect ourselves. By defeating our sisters, we choose to defeat ourselves! Likewise, by keeping our sisters, we choose to keep ourselves. Because I am you and you are me just as she is you and you are she. We are all equal. God intends for us to all be in this together. God knew that sisterhood was a key aspect of successfully surviving and thriving as a woman in this world.

Sisterhood is what God designed us to engage in:
"Be devoted to each other like a loving family. Excel in showing respect for each other" (Romans 12:10 GWT).

If we sit and wait on the next woman or young lady to become our keeper, we risk the chance of it never happening.

The best rule of thumb is for you to initiate the action.

Let's Break the "Sisterhood Cycle of Defeat"!Positivity is contagious. You must understand that the change begins with you. You and every woman or girl reading this book can begin a new sisterhood cycle. Even if you have been the defeater, you can make a positive change for yourself and others.

Take a stand to treat each woman as your sister.

Take a chance to be your sister's keeper!

Miserable Like Me Society

Too many times, women and girls put their business on social media for the world to see. My sister, don't diminish your character to the point of being vain entertainment for others. I've seen many upset women lash out at people for slandering their names. The truth is women slander their own name when they put their business out there. Once you broadcast your personal business out there for others to see and hear, your character is immediately vulnerable for attack. Forget the truth, they can take it however they want. You self-annihilate your own character when you put your business out there for the world to see. Putting your business out there only opens the door for people to assume and make up all kinds of stories about you.

You self-annihilate your own character when you put your business out there for the world to see.

All day long, there are responses to women's posts from other women saying things to confirm what she said and did was right or to tell her how they empathize with her, and how they've been there.

The women respond to her with words like:

"Girl forget these no good baby daddies who won't take care of what they helped to make."

All the responses from other women make her feel like she is validated in what she is going through, but she never even realizes that she's still in the same predicament with no progress. To add insult to injury, she will later have to deal with rumors, lies, and backlashes as a result of putting her business out there. Hear me when I say: those women who respond to your pain and trials are not experts, they are women stuck in the same destructive cycles and are relieved that someone is as miserable or helpless as they are. The majority of them are nosy women who are sitting back with their popcorn watching and screen-shotting your posts while laughing at your despair.

Have you ever really wondered why so many women run to the sight of drama?

They are excited that other women have joined what I call the *"Miserable Like Me Society"*, an invisible club where women are experiencing many hardships with boyfriends, husbands, kids, jobs, finances, and family—and they allegedly support other women who are experiencing the same trials.

However, they are not in a position themselves to help anyone because they don't know how to get help themselves. But the hardships of the other woman make them feel validated—leaving zero amount of help for all of the women.

They all stay down.

They all stay miserable. So, whether they care about your wellbeing or not, it stillstands true that their help is just as vain as you posting your business.

Here's a rule of thumb to live by: Only share your business with those who can help you through your situation or those who can be uplifted by your situation.

The Bible tells us to build each other up by comforting one another (see I Thessalonians 5:11). You should not do things out of anger, for selfish reasons, for validation, or vain purposes. This doesn't look good on you. Moreover, God is not pleased with it.

However, God encourages you to tell your story of how He blessed you, favored you, and brought you out (Psalm 107:2).

Therefore, if it is a testimony and is God-lead, please share it.

For example, there is no positive reason for posting on social media about the lack of child support a woman receives from the father of her children. On the contrary, if she had run into another woman who told her how she struggles as a single mom, this woman could have shared her personal story about how to maintain and overcome the struggle of an absent father. She could even explain on social media how God allowed her to get through it and helped her to be a strong woman and single mother.

The purpose of sharing your business makes a difference regarding your character. Your attitude about things can also determine how far you make it in life. Check your purpose for sharing your business!

I gave you my new definition for *Diva* at the beginning of this book. Once more, a *Diva* (as it relates to this book and your new outlook on life) is a *well-rounded female(s) clothed with dignity, inspiration, vision, achievement, and sisterhood.*

When a *diva* (according to the above definition) crosses paths with other *divas*, they collaboratively display the virtue of sisterhood, and I assure you that it is one powerful force!

I ask you: Your Sisters' Keeper or Defeater?

Which one have you been?

Which one will you aim to be?

19

Survival of the Sisters

ॐ

How do we survive when one of our most infamous obstacles is our own sister? How do we survive in a world where we are considered minority? How do we survive in a society full of disadvantages? The answers to these questions are embedded in sisterhood. But what exactly is sisterhood? From the previous chapter, we are aware that in order to have sisterhood, you must be capable of being your sister's keeper. Let's dig deeper. When I think of sisterhood, the top three qualities that come to mind are *bond, support, and loyalty.*

Bond: The feeling of closeness with your sister.

You should feel a union with her and she should feel that same connection. This is a feeling that ties you together. It doesn't mean you have to be closest friends. It just means that you *share a common attribute*. The bond in a sisterhood is equivalent to the glue within a piece of sculpture. None of the pieces of the sculpture is better than the other. Each part of the sculpture is just as important as the next. Each part is also made up of the same glue. Similar to the sculpture, women should never feel better than the other because each woman is just as important as her sister. In some way, she is made up of the same glue as her sister. The *glue* of sisterhood can be considered as:

Similar struggles, similar financial background, similar upbringing, similar goals, similar successes, or simply being of the same race or gender.

These things make up the bond of sisterhood. It reminds us that we are alike in some way. We are connected on some level. When women and girls feel like they are better than the next or that they should possess more than their sisters, it becomes a competition instead of a sisterhood. All competitions eventually lead to someone losing. If we are always causing our sisters to lose, then how can we as sisters survive? Even if I am not close friends with a woman, when she is in misery, I can always empathize (bond) with her in some way. Whether I have gone through a similar trial as my sister or just the mere fact that we are both women, I feel the glue that connects us. This glue makes us equal. That is the nature of the sisterhood bond.

Support: You uplift her whenever she is feeling low.

When possible, you are there when she needs you. If she has a dream that she wants to pursue, you encourage her. You celebrate her accomplishments with her and you grieve with her during her bad times. If I meet someone along the way with a need, I will support her in any way that I can. It doesn't make a difference that I don't know her too well. There is one woman that I know whom I am not friends with, but the moment I heard of her starting nursing school, I shouted with her. There is another woman I know who was feeling low about being rejected several times from the Master's program at a university. I gave her some words of encouragement from my heart and prayed with her and for her. We weren't the closest of friends, but I saw her as my sister. I didn't smile at her failures. When we see a sister and we have the ability to help her, the virtue of sisterhood tugs on us to offer support toward her.

Loyalty: The feeling that she can trust you.

She doesn't have to fear that you will go behind her back and speak negatively of her. She doesn't have to worry about you ever sharing her secrets with anyone. Loyalty means that you remain true to your sister even in the face of adversity. Even when my friendships with others have deteriorated, I have carried their secrets with me. Sometimes, I forget the secrets. Even when I remember the secrets, no one else will **ever** hear the secrets out of my mouth! Take the higher road even if you have to lose that friendship. **You can lose a friendship without losing sisterhood.**

You Need Her to Survive

Within the sisterhood virtue, you need at least two types of people: a protégé and a mentor. A protégé is a person that you guide, mentor, and have a positive influence over. The protégé is usually a younger person. However, whether younger or older, this is a person that you support and mentor in an area that you are very experienced in. Although you may lack in some areas, there is at least *one* positive thing that you do well. For example, you may be a person that knows how to cook well and overhear someone at your job or in your church that would like to learn. You could take that person under your wings and teach them. In doing so, you will be engaging in sisterhood by supporting her. When we are able to help others in ways that we never knew we could, we gain a sense of fulfillment.

We feel a purpose in life.

Additionally, you learn a few things while teaching others because God's Spirit directs you. I cannot tell you how many times I have mentored others whereby I have also grown in the process of helping them. The reason is because God is working on us when we take our minds off of ourselves and place our minds on someone else. It's something about the unselfish act of doing for others even in the midst of our adversities and deficiencies that makes God smile. So, take time to find a protégé. Whoever she is, you need her. Seek God for guidance, and engage in Sisterhood leadership. Somewhere during the process of finding a protégé, please be sure to get a mentor. The sisterhood virtue works both ways. In order to be any type of leader, you must be able to follow. Don't be intimidated; be empowered because whoever the mentor is, you need her. *By all means, please pick someone that lives a Godly lifestyle to mentor you.* You need her to survive.

There's a song by Hezekiah Walker [1] that goes:

I need you. You need me.

We're all a part of God's body.

Stand with me. Agree with me...

You are important to me...

I won't harm you with words from my mouth...

I love you. I need you to survive...

This song reminds us that we are interdependent. Sisterhood should be viewed as being one big body of many women and girls working together, depending on each other, and respecting each other to make the body function properly. Sisterhood is deteriorating because we are not behaving as one body. The Bible tells us that God gave each woman her own functions. He gave each of us our own capabilities. This means that my gift or capability may be different from yours, but we need each other to keep sisterhood alive.

> "And the eye cannot say unto the hand, I have no need of thee: nor again the head to the feet, I have no need of you" (I Corinthians 12:21).

This scripture eradicates every fallacy stated by a person that claims she doesn't need anybody. No single person makes up the entire body of sisterhood. **Just as it takes a village to raise one child, it takes a multitude of Divas to generate a thriving sisterhood.** The Bible also tells us that the arm cannot do the function of the leg. God has given you strengths. He has also given strengths to your sister. "If the whole body were an eye, how would you hear? Or if your whole body were an ear, how would you smell anything" (I Corinthians 12:17 NLT)? In other words, if God gave every single woman the same ability, nothing would get done. This is the reason that your sister has a capability or "strength" that you don't have and vice versa. This is also the reason that we should not get jealous of our sisters. We should applaud them. We teach them what we know and we learn what we do not know from them.

Interdependency. This is God's intention.

Finally, the Bible tells us that we are to hurt when our sisters hurt and rejoice when our sisters rejoice (see I Corinthians 12:26). That feeling of happiness that women get when they see another woman fall is not healthy; it's not Godly and it's not a trait of sisterhood. When a woman laughs and smiles at her sister's adversities, it reveals some hidden dysfunction within herself. Let's work on refraining from knocking down our own sisters. It makes my soul so happy when I see black women succeeding in life!

With the biggest smile, I say to myself, "Look at my sister! *We're* winning!" We need to uplift our sisters, assist them, and learn from those that we can. Pray for your sister and watch how God changes things for you. Acknowledge the need for your sister and watch you and your sisters shoot to success!

20

Sister Power

ॐ

Are you friends with someone who is always at war with other females? If so, run the other way. A woman with sound values, who would not normally speak negatively about others, respects her elders, and values education; finds herself hanging around friends who are disrespectful. Her friends have no desire for education or legitimate success, and they spread rumors all the time. She feels as if their bad characters have nothing to do with her because after all, that's not who *she* is. Wrong! Their bad characters have a lot to do with her because she is associated with them. Therefore, when she signed up to hang with them, she also signed up to have a similar reputation as them. Employers, teachers, guys, and females identify her as a disrespectful, uncaring, trouble-making female with a lack of values just like her friends. If your friends are not doing anything with their lives, it's more than likely that they are distractions to you. In order to stay focused, makes friends with someone who can help you succeed. Say your farewells to those who tend to distract you from your goals.

"Don't be misled: Bad company corrupts good character" (I Corinthians 15:33). Too much negative energy will stick to you like Velcro. This is especially the case when you are attempting to improve your life, values, or goals. For example, if your mind is on marriage and you constantly hang around a lot of women who still love to party and date multiple guys, you will be bombarded with comments that are contrary to your goals and values.

They will say things like:

"Girl, I'm not getting married. Nobody does that anymore."

"Single women have more fun! No man is going to tell me what to do!"

"Forever is a long time! Men change when they get married."

"Girl please, marriage is overrated and so is love."

You may even be bombarded with conversations about other women with failed marriages. Even if they are not trying to discourage you, you cannot stop your mind from hearing and receiving that poison. Therefore, you should stay away from people that are not on the same page as you. People that are not married cannot accurately tell you how the married life is. Those with different mindsets than you will still speak negatively about things you feel positively about. This can lead to discouragement. If their mindset is not on success in the way that your mind is, their communication will be different from yours. In fact, their words can be like poison to your aspirations or goals. No matter how strong-minded you are, the constant, worldly, small-minded communication of friends will begin to stick in your mind and war against you. Satan works in our minds. Likewise, just because God tells us to love everyone and desires for us to treat everyone as sisters does *not* mean we are to be best friends with everyone. In fact, the bible even warns us that bad company can ruin us. Therefore, I recommend that you maintain your sisterhood without being naïve about friendships. Know the difference between sisterhood and friendship. In fact, you should not have a massive amount of close friends because that can easily become a disaster. *Where there is a zoo full of animals, you are bound to find snakes. Likewise, where there is a massive circle of friends; some are bound to be sneaky, treacherous, and full of hidden agendas.*

It's hard to have time for Jesus as a friend when we have to divide so much of our time between the slews of friends that we have. Besides, I like not having my name in drama. I also like not having to hear what I've said being repeated by someone that I did not tell. The truth is the more friends you have, the more chaotic your life can be. A couple of close friends are plenty company, but too many close friends can equal chaos, confusion, and conflicts. Therefore, I urge you to show sisterhood to all women, but limit the amount of women you allow in your *close* friendship circle.

Same Power, Different Ladder

As a woman, you have the same power that any other woman has. You just have to realize it and tap into it. Remember that everyone has a mountain to climb just as everyone has a ladder designed to get them to the top. *If women would stop focusing on pulling our sisters off their ladders, it would free up so much energy to climb to the top of their own ladders.* Since you have your own ladder, you should not push your sister off the ladder that she is using to climb to success. Grab your own ladder so that you can excel just like your sister. Ecclesiastes 4:9 reads, "Two people are better off than one, for they can help each other succeed" (NLT). Don't be intimidated by the woman with more than you. Whether they have more finances, more materialistic things, more education, more favor, or more anointing, they can help you get to where you desire to be. No matter the height or the weight, no *one* person is ever stronger than the two people together. To translate, no matter how strong, smart, or ambitious you are; when you engage in sisterhood, you can become even more ambitious, wiser, and stronger. I cannot say it enough: we defeat ourselves when we defeat our sisters.

Our Sisters' Many Names

"I'm a Bad Bitch!" "What's up Bitch?!"
"That's my day one Bitch right there!"

I know I know! Everybody says the 'B' word, right?
Women and girls don't mean anything negative when they refer to their best friend as the 'B' word, right? They don't intend on saying that their sister is promiscuous when they call her a whore. And calling themselves the 'B' word does no harm to themselves. Or, so they think. In some kind of way, women and girls view this as a type of love for their sisters. Satan is a liar! He is a great at his craft, which includes being a deceiver who has conned our sisters into believing that name calling is harmless to our souls and future. Quite the contrary!

"The tongue can bring death or life; those who love to talk will reap the consequences" (Proverbs 18:21 NLT).

Exactly what is a 'bitch'? We know the original definition of the word is a female dog. Merriam-Webster dictionary also tells us that the definition of the word 'bitch' is:

1. A lewd (rude) or ***immoral*** woman.
2. A malicious, spiteful, or overbearing woman.
3. Something that is extremely difficult, objectionable, or unpleasant.

It's no surprise that our sisterhood is rapidly diminishing!

It's no wonder we have so many women **with no morals**, who are rude, obnoxious, loud, messy, petty, full of drama, ruthless, and more! We go around speaking and receiving negative things into our own personalities without even noticing it! That's Satan's tactic. He wants us to think the words are meaningless so that we are totally oblivious to our own self-imposed failures. The next thing you know, women are wondering why they cannot keep a job, get offered a good career, have a great man who treats them well, stay in relationships, or maintain healthy friendships.

The very first definition of the word "bitch" is a woman with no morals. What employer wants a lady with little or no morals? What *decent* man wants a woman **with no morals for herself** or one who is bossy, over the top, very difficult to deal with, and doesn't know how to be meek even if it was written on the palm of her hand? What right-minded, upright, *dignified* woman wants a friend who is always offensive and rude? It sounds harsh, but these are all the definitions of a bitch that we speak on ourselves and our sisters. It's high time that we and our sisters be unchained from this cycle of self-destruction. **Satan's**

demons take on the negativity that you speak. God's angels take on the positivity that you speak when it is in line with His will. Stop giving ourselves and our sisters these degrading names. Choose to reject every degrading name thrown at you and speak life over yourself.

Remember how I told you that hurt sisters hurt other sisters and the hurt eventually comes back around? The same thing applies for the positivity. Empowered sisters empower others, which ultimately comes back around. In order to empower your sisters, you must do the following:

1. Stay true to the 3 qualities of sisterhood: bond, support, and loyalty.
2. Refrain from gossip.
3. Find a protégé and a mentor.
4. Limit your friendship circle while showing sisterhood to all women.
5. Refrain from the sister name-calling.

It's time to take a stand for sisterhood. It's time to empower her! Once you do, the empowerment will soon be returned to you from another sister. You are now aware of the statistics and strongholds against black women. We are sisters. Let's empower each other! The power of a black woman when successively combined with the power of another black woman makes a mighty force!

A Letter to My Father

Daddy,

The things you took me through literally almost killed me. I realize now that it was Satan using you to work mightily against my destiny. I realize that you allowed him to use you. I realize that God allowed me to be slain so that I could be the hope for many in chains. I'm grateful for the good and the painful. I don't regret you and I don't regret the calling on my life. I carry this cross for the Kingdom of God. I've been healed and set free, and was able to forgive the imperfect part of you. Forgiving you blessed me. I know you knew this, but I'll say it one more time: I forgive you for it all daddy. I love you very much in spite of it all. I prayed for you daily until God called you home.

Rest peacefully daddy,
Nique

ABOUT THE AUTHOR

DR. NIOKA SMITH, LCPC, MFT

Dr. Nioka Smith is a Licensed Clinical Christian Counselor, Marriage and Family Therapist, Certified Christian Life Coach, Inspirational Speaker, and Licensed Educator. She is the Chief Executive Officer of J. Kenkade Publishing® and runs a Counseling practice called Dr. Nioka Smith Counseling. She is also the Founder and President of DIVAS Unchained, LLC®, a national empowerment society for women and girls.

She has a divine purpose and gift for women and girls who are discouraged, stagnant, hurting, or stuck in bad relationship cycles, as well as those who just need a little boost to get ahead in life. She specializes in stress/anxiety/depression, sexual abuse recovery, marriage and family, and life recovery. She has a burning passion to help women and girls heal from their past as well as recognize and achieve their full potential in all areas of life.

Dr. Nioka holds a Doctoral Degree in Christian Counseling, a Master's Degree in Education, and a Bachelor's Degree in Speech Communication. She describes herself as a woman of many gifts with an anointing and a heart for God's people; a trailblazer, a true inspiration to many, relatable, and understanding. She is a virtuous wife and proud mother of three. Dr. Nioka has more books in her spirit that she is soon to write and release. Be on the lookout! Follow her on social media: @drniokasmith

Book Dr. Nioka!

Available for

WORKSHOPS

SEMINARS

CONFERENCES

FACILITATING AND HOSTING EVENTS

LIFE COACHING

COUNSELING

TRAINING FOR EDUCATORS
& MINISTRY LEADERS

Website: www.drniokasmith.com
Email: info@drniokasmith.com
Phone: (501) 891-6745
YouTube, Facebook & Instagram: @drniokasmith

Dr. Nioka would love to hear how this book helped you.
Please send your testimony via email or social media.

To request a *signed* copy of "DIVAS Unchained", visit
www.drniokasmith.com or call (501) 891-6745.

Shop with Us!

www.drniokasmith.com/shop

KING.
LEADER.
PROVIDER.
PROTECTOR.
BLACK MAN.
NOT GUILTY.

QUEEN.
SURVIVOR.
RESILIENT.
EMPOWERED.
FAVORED &
UNAPOLOGETIC.

Respect MY WORTH

I'M A STATISTIC
BREAKING
STRONGHOLD
BREAKING
Diva

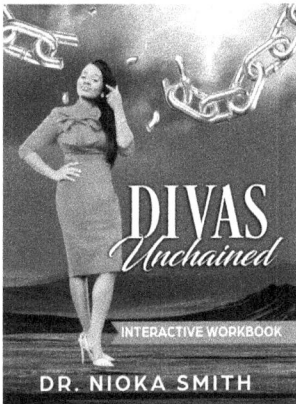

Send Mail to:
Dr. Nioka Smith Counseling, LLC
6104 Forbing Rd.
Little Rock, AR, 72209

Email to:
info@drniokasmith.com

ACKNOWLEDGMENTS

To my husband Coral,
I would not have finished this book if it was not for your amazing support and encouragement throughout the entire writing process. Thank you for always believing in me even when I didn't believe in myself. You have a special way of bringing out the best in me. You've always cherished my worth and treated me like a queen. You've been my rock during the hardest times of my life. You are my king, the love of my life, and my best friend. I love you with my soul.

To my mother Mary,
You've taught me so much that I will carry with me for the rest of my life. Thank you for teaching me dignity, endurance, selfless love, and humility. Thank you for introducing me to Jesus and for instilling such a rich spiritual foundation within me. Everything that I am; everything that I've achieved is because of God and you. I love you my queen.

To Apostle Kingsley Eruemulor,
God sent me to you at the most pivotal point in my life. It was either die from my strongholds or live and *fight* for the power within me. Your fire-filled anointing helped break the strongest yokes in my life. I was in chains, but through God and His powerful anointing within you, I was healed and delivered from years of spiritual bondage. I thank you always for being my Spiritual father. I love you.

To Bishop Melvin Jackson,
When I was experiencing the most violent storms at the hands of my daddy, your powerful preaching and leadership kept me hopeful and grounded. There were times I thought I would die at home, but I found a safe place in the presence of God at New Beginnings Church. Thank you for being an instrumental part of my spiritual roots.

To Pastor Kevin & Lady Regina Wiley,
Your inspiration reaches deep. You have been a blessing to my family. Thank you for all of your words of encouragement and words of wisdom throughout the years.

To Minister Charles & Stephanie Archer,
Thank you for always supporting me. I love you.

To my son Jabari,
Your life helped change my life in so many extraordinary ways. Your birth marked the beginning of this remarkable new journey. Never forget that you are Greatness. You are my pride and my world.

To my daughters Kennedi and Kadence,
To whom this book is dedicated. When this fast paced world becomes too much pressure, always remember that your mighty power is from above you and your amazing worth is within you. I do this for you. My heart beats for you.

To my siblings Shekila, Keith, Rahsaan, and Tichina,
Thanks for being such an integral part of my support system. From helping with my kids to supporting me during the biggest moments of my life. Even in the midst of all the trials we've been through in our lives, two things have always remained: our love and bond. You are four of the most important people in my life! I love you beyond eternity.

To my grandparents Pearl and Ezell,
Thanks to the both of you for being a big part of my mother's village for us. I'll never forget all that you've done for me. Your home was always an escape from the real world. Grandma, you are the backbone of my backbone and the queen of my queen. I'll always be your Nikki. I love you.

To Jesus Christ, my Creator, Savior, and Strong tower,
Thank you for keeping me! Thank you for choosing me!

-Dr. Nioka *"PeculiarChild"* Smith
I Peter 2:9

References

CHAPTER 4: PART II CLOSED LEGS DON'T GET FED

1. (1997). Whatever happened to childhood? The problem of teen pregnancy in the united states. National Campaign to Prevent Teen Pregnancy. Washington DC.
2. U.S. Census Bureau-Table C2. (2014). Household relationship and living arrangements of children under 18 years, by age and sex.
3. U.S. Census Bureau-Table C8. (2014). Poverty status, food stamp receipt, and public assistance for children under 18 years by selected characteristics.

CHAPTER 5: WIFE ME DOWN

1. Quoted by Maya Angelou. Accessed at http://www.goodreads.com/ author/ quotes/3503.Maya_Angelou.
2. Jayson, S. (2012). Nearly 40% of women today have never been married. USA Today. Retrieved from http://usatoday30.usatoday.com/news/health/wellness/story/2012-03-22/Nearly-40-of-women-today-have-never-been-married/53697418/1.
3. National Women's Law Center. (2000-2013). Poverty & Income Among Women & Families.
4. (2013). U.S. marriage rate is lowest in more than 100 years. HealthDay Consumer News Service.

CHAPTER 6: LIFE'S LEMONS

1. Virginia Coalition for Prevention of Child Abuse. Retrieved from http://alexandria-va.gov/uploadedFiles/women/info/DVP6%20CHILD.pdf.
2. Bowker, L. H., Arbitell, M., & McFerron,J. R. (1988). On the relationship between wife beating and child abuse. Perspectives on Wife Abuse. Newbury Park, CA: Sage.
3. Noll, J. G., Shenk, C. E., & Putnam, K. T. (2009). Childhood sexual abuse and adolescent pregnancy: a meta-analytic update. Journal of Pediatric Psychology, 34, 366-378.
4. World Health Organization. (2002). Retrieved from Rainn: Rape, Abuse, & Incest National Network. https://rainn.org/getinformation/statistics/sexual-assault-victims.

CHAPTER 7: LEMONS TO LEMONADE

1. When girls don't graduate, we all fail: A call to improve high school graduation rates (2007). National Women's Law Center (NWLC). Retrieved from http://www.nwlc.org/sites/default/files/pdfs/when_girls_dont_graduate.pdf.
2. Hayes, J. & Hartmann, H. (2011). Women and men living on the edge: Economic insecurity after the great recession. Institute for Women's Policy Research/Rockefeller Survey of Economic Security. Can be accessed at www.iwpr.org/publications.
3. Vespa, J., Lewis, J.M., & Kreider, R. M. (2013). America's families and living arrangements: 2012, current population reports. U.S. Census Bureau, Washington DC. Retrieved from http://www.census.gov/prod/2013pubs/p20-570.pdf.
4. Gilliam Jr, F. D. (1999). The welfare queen experiment: How viewers react to images of African-American mothers on welfare. Nieman Foundation for Journalism at Harvard: Nieman Reports. Retrieved from http://www.nieman.harvard.edu/reports/article/102223/ The-Welfare-Queen-Experiment.aspx.
5. Bulimia Eating Disorders. The shocking statistics that abuse leaves in its wake. Retrieved from http://www.bulimiaeatingdisorders.com/shocking_statistics.php.

CHAPTER 8: BREAKING THE CHAINS OF STRONGHOLDS

1. Child Abuse Solutions. Retrieved from centerforjudicialexcellence.org.
2. Roesler, T. A. MD & Wind, T.A. (1994). Telling the secret: adult women describe their disclosure of incest. Journal of Interpersonal Violence, 9, 327-338.

CHAPTER 9: THE GIFTED CRY

1. Buchanan, A. (2011). Go with the flow. Women's Health, 8 (2).

2. Sapp, M. (2007). Place of worship. On Thirsty [CD]. Zomba Recording, LLC.

CHAPTER 10: DARE TO INSPIRE

1. RELAYHEALTH (2013). SUICIDE IN CHILDREN AND TEENS. CRS-PEDIATRIC ADVISOR.

CHAPTER 11: THE FACE OF CONFIDENCE

1. Confidence Coalition. Retrieved from http://www.confidencecoalition.org/assets/1442/8-2-13_facts_on_cc_2013.pdf?1377879930152.

CHAPTER 12: A WALK FROM MIRRORS TO WINDOWS

1. Family Facts. Marriage and poverty. The Heritage Foundation. Retrieved from http://www.familyfacts.org/briefs/8/marriage-and-poverty.

2. The national campaign to prevent teen and unplanned pregnancy. http://stayteen.org/teen-pregnancy

3. Bulimia Eating Disorders. The shocking statistics that abuse leaves in its wake. Retrieved from http://www.bulimiaeatingdisorders.com/shocking_statistics.php.

CHAPTER 13: WRITE THE VISION

1. Definition retrieved from Dictionary.reference.com/browse/vision.

CHAPTER 14: NOTHING COMES TO SLEEPERS BUT A DREAM

1. Campbell, E. & Campbell, T. (2008). Get up [Recorded by Mary Mary]. On The Sound [CD]. Columbia Records.

2. Quote accessed at http://www.goodreads.com/quotes/381189-nothing-comes-to-a-sleeper-but-a-dream-wake-up.

CHAPTER 15: MICROWAVE GENERATION

1. Agnew, T. & Robinson, K. Thoughts of a savage. The microwave generation: I want it all now. Jenesis Magazine. Retrieved at http://www.jenesismagazine.com/thoughts-of-a-savage-the- microwave-generation-i-want-it-all-now/.

2. Low Wage Work. Facts about Low Wage Work. Retrieved from http://www.low-wagework.org/facts-about-low-wage-work.html.

3. Family Facts. Marriage and poverty. The Heritage Foundation. Retrieved from http://www.familyfacts.org/briefs/8/marriage-and-poverty.

CHAPTER 16: SUCCEED ON PURPOSE

1. Quoted by Maya Angelou. Accessed at http://www.goodreads.com/author/quotes/3503.Maya_Angelou.

2. Quoted by Benjamin Franklin. Accessed at http://www.goodreads.com/quotes/460142-if-you-fail-to-plan-you-are-planning-to-fail.

3. When girls don't graduate, we all fail: A call to improve high school graduation rates (2007). National Women's Law Center (NWLC). Retrieved from http://www.nwlc.org/sites/default/files/pdfs/when_girls_dont_graduate.pdf.

4. Quoted by Gordon B. Hinckley. Accessed at http://www.goodreads.com/quotes/24571-mediocrity-will-never-do-you-are-capable-of-something-better.

5. Hayes, J. & Hartmann, H. (2011). Women and men living on the edge: Economic insecurity after the great recession. Institute for Women's Policy Research/Rockefeller Survey of Economic Security. Can be accessed at www.iwpr.org/publications.

7. Quoted by Donny Miller. Accessed at http://www.goodreads.com/ quotes/527168-in-the-age-of-information-ignorance-is-a-choice.

CHAPTER 17: THE GREATEST ACHIEVEMENT OF ALL

1. Campbell, E. & Campbell, T. (2012). God in me [Mary Mary]. On Go Get It [CD]. New York, NY: Columbia Records.

CHAPTER 19: SURVIVAL OF THE SISTERS

1. Walker, H. & The Love Fellowship Choir (2002). I need you to survive. On Family Affair II Live at Radio City Music Hall [CD]. Verity Records.

J. Kenkade
PUBLISHING®

www.ingramcontent.com/pod-product-compliance
Lightning Source LLC
Chambersburg PA
CBHW062149080426
42734CB00010B/1614